Starting Out in Project Management

Starting Out in Project Management

Third edition

Association for Project Management

Association for Project Management
Ibis House, Regent Park
Summerleys Road, Princes Risborough
Buckinghamshire
HP27 9LE

First published 2004
Second edition 2007
Third edition 2018

British Library Cataloguing in Publication Data is available.
Paperback ISBN: 978-1-903494-72-1
eISBN: 978-1-903494-73-8

Cover design by Fountainhead Creative Consultants
Typeset by RefineCatch Limited, Bungay, Suffolk
in 11/14pt Foundry Sans

Contents

Contents

Contents

List of figures

Foreword

As a modern, professional body, we recognise the need to develop talent for the future by ensuring that the next generation of project manager is equipped with the core skills required and given clear guidance and support throughout their career journey.

Since its release in 2004 *Starting Out in Project Management* has built a deserved reputation as the 'go-to guide' for those new to project management. The text is easy-to-follow and the diagrams are easy-to-understand. In fact, it's an easy read from start to finish.

The latest edition builds on that success and is sure to reward anybody who is curious to learn more, for example, not just about the time, cost, quality triangle, but the project manager's trilemma in trying to balance them.

Starting Out is written as an introductory text, as a good general read, as a reference book – and as an enduring source of inspiration for any aspiring project manager.

Association for Project Management–
the chartered body for the project profession

January 2018

Preface

When we wrote the first edition of this book in 2003, our respective children Amy, Kirsty, Joel, Megan, Lois (Simon) and Josh and Helen (Murray-Webster) were all in either university or school (or pre-school) and project management was struggling to break out of its traditional roots and into the modern world of business and fast-moving organisational change. The second edition, published 10 years ago in 2007 was updated slightly, but progress in modernising project management was slow. We are delighted with the sales of that book and it is our privilege to be asked to write this third edition. What is really pleasing for us is to see project management coming of age as an essential, business-critical discipline, and a chartered profession. More amazing has been to watch our children and their partners move either directly or indirectly into the world of project management and put into practice the profession that has served us well and that we care so much about. It is with particular pride too that we can attribute the modernised figures for this edition to Josh Murray-Webster. Until the fourth edition . . .

Peter Simon
Ruth Murray-Webster

Fundamental features of project management

Introduction

In this section we discuss some of the main concepts that underpin **project management**. These include the recognition that **projects** are different from **business-as-usual**, and that alongside projects we have other mechanisms for delivering planned change called **programmes** and **portfolios**.

We will also discuss the key roles needed to ensure that projects are successfully delivered. These include the **sponsor** and **project manager** who work with the **project team** and with business users to deliver a project, **reporting** to a **steering group/committee**. We touch on the ways an organisation can set itself up to deliver projects, recognising that different arrangements suit different situations.

The idea of a **project life cycle** is the key differentiator between projects and business-as-usual. All projects follow a **life cycle** of some description, and we will outline the basic ideas of a project life cycle and of the **extended** and **product life cycles**.

Finally, projects are delivered by people and an ability to lead teams, negotiate and resolve conflicts is a vital skill, so we outline the basic elements of **teamwork**, leadership, conflict management and negotiation.

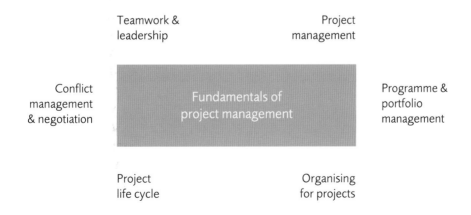

Figure 1.1 Fundamentals of project management – overview

1

Project management

Projects and project management

Projects and project management have been around for a very long time. Some of the iconic buildings and structures we all know were created over 5,000 years ago and it is clear that they could not have been constructed without a great deal of planning and organisation. However, the discipline of project management as we know it today has been around not nearly so long. Many argue that it is less than 50 years old (from the time of the North Sea oil boom and the first major nuclear power stations), while others suggest that it is more like 100 years. Henry Gantt of 'Gantt chart' fame published his book *Organizing for Work* in 1919. It doesn't really matter when it all started. What is important is that in today's fast-moving world the successful delivery of projects has never been more important.

What is a project?

At its simplest level the word project is used to describe activities that are done to meet specific **objectives** for change. Changes that are managed as projects can be amendments to things that already exist, or the introduction of new things. It can involve new products, new services, or improvement to existing products or services. Whatever the cause of the change and the nature of the project, the principles of project management always apply.

Even though project work involves doing new things, it still needs to be controlled, so that the specific objectives are met and the organisation actually gains the desired **benefits**. One way that this control is achieved is by setting targets or **constraints** for time, cost and **quality**. Some people and some organisations prefer to use the term performance rather than quality. For a 'starting out' book we can use the terms quality and performance interchangeably, both meaning that the project needs to meet defined stakeholder **requirements**. When we talk about **stakeholders** in project management, we mean the organisations or people who have an interest or role in the work, or are impacted by it.

Project work is rarely ever done within a single part of an organisation, e.g. contained within one department or using a single specialist group. Project work cuts across traditional boundaries and requires people to come together temporarily to focus on achieving the specific project objectives. As a result, effective teamwork is central to projects.

Doing new things means that the project's **outputs**, **outcomes** and/or benefits can never be predicted with certainty. Uncertain situations are all around us, but the nature of project work means that there tends to be lots of uncertainty that might affect the project. For example, it is not possible to know with any degree of certainty how long it will take to create a new design; or to build something that uses new technology. Likewise, it is not possible to know if a team who have not worked together before will be effective, or whether a new product, e.g. a Formula One racing car, will perform until it is actually tested, or whether a new smart phone will sell in the numbers expected. The fact that projects are uncertain means that project managers need to clearly understand the underpinning **assumptions** being made by stakeholders, and actively manage risk throughout the life of the project.

All of the points made so far help define project work as distinct from other sorts of work. Most organisations will be able to separate those tasks that are done to maintain the business-as-usual or operational activities from those things that are done to introduce change, i.e. projects (and programmes).

Projects and business-as-usual

The main way in which projects are different from the routine business of work is associated with the uniqueness of projects. While routine work involves the repetition of processes in a way that gives consistency and reliability, project work involves doing new things, or modifying existing methods and practices. This means that project work, unlike business-as-usual, will always have a defined start and an end point, and a particular and unique scope of work to do between those points.

Taking all these considerations together, projects can be said to have the following features:

- unique endeavour with defined start and finish points
- undertaken to achieve specific objectives for change
- carried out within defined time, cost and quality constraints

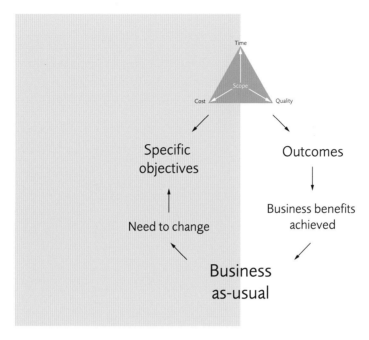

Figure 1.2 Projects and business-as-usual

- requires team-working across traditional departmental boundaries
- delivers outputs that enable outcomes to the business that are beneficial
- necessarily involves **risk** that needs to be managed.

Business-as-usual does not meet these criteria.

Project Children's Hospice (PCH)

You have been approached by a friend to be part of an initiative to raise funds for your local children's hospice. You work in the headquarters building of a company along with 500 other people. Your friend would like you to organise a fund-raising event to take place during normal working hours in exactly 10 weeks' time. This coincides with a number of other fundraising initiatives that will be happening for the same cause on the same day. Your initial objectives are to involve as many people as possible and to raise at least £10,000 for the charity.

7

Project management

If projects are used to introduce change, it follows that project management is primarily about organising and controlling the introduction of the desired change.

The words or phrases that tend to be used to describe project management include:

- understanding the needs and requirements of all the stakeholders
- planning what work needs to be done, when, by whom and to what standards
- building and motivating the team to achieve the planned work
- coordinating the work of a range of different people
- monitoring that the work is being done to plan (time, cost and quality/ performance)
- taking action to keep the planned work on track, or to change the plan in a controlled way if that is the best way to achieve the change objectives
- delivering successful results (outputs, outcomes and/or benefits).

Project management should be a service to the organisation that is requesting the change, and is the process by which control is exerted over the project in order to achieve a desired end point.

Some projects have a dedicated project manager who takes responsibility for delivering the project objectives to time, cost and quality. Where this is the case

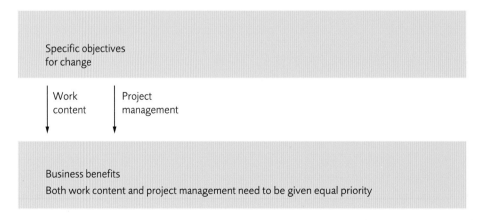

Specific objectives
for change

Work content | Project management

Business benefits
Both work content and project management need to be given equal priority

Figure 1.3 Balancing managing and doing

it will be easy to see that the work the project manager does is focused on the points in the bulleted list above.

Some projects have a project manager who additionally takes on the role of a technical specialist within the project team, e.g. a business analyst who is both managing the project to establish feasibility for a new computer system, and doing the business analysis themselves, or a manager of a hockey team who is both managing the organisation of a major tournament and playing in the tournament on the day.

When this happens – and it does all the time when projects are small or contained primarily within one part of the organisation – it is really important that the project manager focuses just as much on the *management* of the project as on *completing the work* that must be done for the project to be a success.

Project Children's Hospice (PCH)

You are the project manager for Project Children's Hospice (PCH). It is your responsibility to plan what needs to be done, making use of as many of the staff members as is practical. As you are an expert in communications management, you will probably design and carry out the communications element of the project yourself. It is clearly your responsibility to monitor the work as it progresses, as well as motivate and coordinate your project team.

Project management processes

Processes are things that turn inputs into outputs.

It follows, then, that **project management processes** turn inputs, including things such as user requirements or technical specifications, into those outputs that will achieve the specific change objectives, e.g. new products or services.

Project management processes include:

- a starting or initiating process that secures agreement to begin a portion of work
- a planning process that takes an input and turns it into a set of integrated plans against which to implement the project. As the project progresses there is

invariably a need for a re-planning process to reflect project progress or changes in objectives

- a monitoring process that measures the progress of a project against its plan, whether it is ahead or behind schedule, over-spending or under-spending against budget, or delivering outputs that meet the desired performance or quality objectives
- a controlling process that reacts to the information gathered during monitoring, and enables decisions to be made to correct lateness, over-spending or poor quality
- a learning process that takes an input such as a finished project and turns it into a set of amended guidelines, processes and checklists for the next project
- a closing process that formally concludes a portion of work.

You will see a pattern among these processes. They are not specific to any particular project or any project phase; rather, they are the things that happen on all projects and in all phases of a project. They are the things concerned with project management in general, rather than any specific project.

The labels and terms used to describe a particular project process may vary. Sometimes it is easy to become confused between the labels given for project management processes and the labels given for the phases in a project life cycle. This will be explored further in Chapter 4, which deals specifically with the project life cycle.

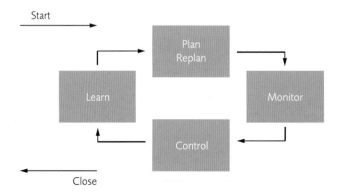

Figure 1.4 Project management processes

The fact is, theoretical terms rarely matter. What does matter in practice is that you not only understand the terms that are used in your organisation, but also that you can compare and contrast them with other terms used in published literature about project management as a means of understanding what your organisation does and why.

Project Children's Hospice (PCH)

Your project to raise money for the children's hospice charity is made up of four distinct phases: concept, definition, development and handover and closure. These phases make up the life cycle for your project.

To apply project management processes, each phase needs to be started, planned, monitored, controlled and closed, having learned any lessons for future projects.

PCH day will take place in exactly 10 weeks. This date is not moveable. You have talked to your boss who is the HR director. She supports the project and has agreed to act as sponsor but has introduced the following new constraints, within which you must manage the project:

- Whatever you do must not offend anyone.
- The whole project must not eat up more than 1,000 hours of work time for staff, including you.
- There should be no more than £500 of external expenditure.
- The company should get good press through local newspaper, radio and TV coverage.

The relationship between time, cost and quality

Time, cost and quality are the three attributes that are typically described as either objectives or constraints for any project. For example:

- The project must be completed by 31 December 2020.
- The project must not spend more than £500,000.
- The products and services created must meet specification X456.

Sometimes these attributes are alternatively stated as schedule, budget and performance, but here we will refer to time, cost and quality. The relationship between these three attributes is at the heart of project management.

It is unlikely that any project could ever achieve objectives that are considered to be the quickest, the cheapest and the best, even though that is what we would all like. In fact, if a project has to be delivered to meet a challenging finish date, it is likely that it will cost the organisation more overall than if it had a more relaxed schedule. Likewise, if a project has to achieve a tight specification for quality, it will probably cost more or take longer than it would have if the quality requirements had been reduced.

Projects are intended to be planned taking the relative priorities of time, cost and quality into account at the start, but given the challenges of estimating and the inherent uncertainties within projects, it is perhaps no surprise that projects need to adjust over time and that (for example) projects involving public safety end up taking longer and costing more than originally planned because, during delivery, quality is given greater priority than time and cost. Similarly, projects that need to be completed by a certain date, perhaps building a new stadium for a planned sporting event, almost invariably cost more than planned and/or have a finished product that is to a lower specification than was originally conceived.

Projects are unique, and initial plans that reflect time, cost and quality objectives are, in reality, 'educated guesses' that need to be implemented in an uncertain world. In such a scenario, it is rare for the project to proceed exactly to plan. The more usual situation is that something happens that requires the project manager to make a 'trade-off' – to take more time to achieve the specification, to spend more money to hold the deadline, or to agree reduced quality in order to hold the time and cost plans.

Because such dilemmas typify project management, the triangular relationship between time, cost and quality is often called the 'iron triangle of project management' or the 'project manager's trilemma'.

Often the area inside the triangle is said to represent the project **scope**, i.e. all the work that has to be done to achieve the time, cost and quality objectives. This is clearly another attribute of the project that can be varied as long as the project manager can be certain that an amended scope will still deliver the outcomes and benefits that the organisation requires from the change. A reduction in scope means that less work will be done, which then makes time and cost objectives more achievable. Sometimes there is a confusion between scope and quality. Scope defines the outputs of the project. Outputs are usually physical things, such as a document, a wall or a pump. Quality defines the grade or specification

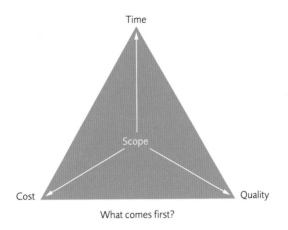

Figure 1.5 The project manager's trilemma

that the project outputs (the document, wall or pump in this example) need to be delivered to. Some parts of the scope (outputs) can be less tangible, such as changes in behaviour of staff. In this case defining quality can be more difficult but is still required.

It follows, then, that the most important thing for a project manager to understand when balancing the time, cost and quality objectives is the relative priority of objectives for the client organisation. Is it more important to finish on time, on budget or to the right quality?

Project Children's Hospice (PCH)

For Project Children's Hospice you understand the relative priorities to be: first, time, because the date is fixed; second, cost, because your boss has given you an effective maximum budget; and third, quality (in terms of positive awareness generated and funds raised), as no promises have been made to the national charity.

2

Programme management and portfolio management

Programmes and portfolios

The words programme and portfolio have multiple meanings both in general and in business. It is therefore important to understand what these terms mean in relation to project management. Both programmes and portfolios are each distinct from projects, and many people working on projects in organisations will recognise that their project is part of a wider programme or portfolio. It follows then that understanding what programmes and portfolios are, and what they are meant to achieve, is important background for those starting out in project management.

What is a programme and what is programme management?

Programme is a collective term either for a group of projects, or for a group of projects and change management activities, that together achieve a beneficial change of a strategic nature. A few years ago, the word *programme* was used to describe any collection of projects, but thinking has now moved on to clearly differentiate between projects, programmes and portfolios. Portfolios will be described in the next section.

A programme is not just a large project. In a large project, such as designing and building a high speed railway system or designing and building a sports stadium, it is possible to identify all the work to be done at the start, even if that work will take many years to complete. The work is not optional; to achieve the stated specification all the work needs to be done.

In a programme, such as the merger of two companies or a major restructuring of a business, it is possible to focus on the end goal, but it is not possible at the outset to identify all the work that will need to be done to get there. Projects will be planned and delivered in time-phased 'chunks' (usually called **tranches**) and when the business goals (outcomes and benefits) have been achieved, work will stop. Programmes are much more ambiguous than projects, and **programme management** involves some different skills from project management.

Programme management involves coordinating work across multiple projects and business-as-usual in order to bring about beneficial change, usually of a strategic nature, for an organisation.

This description suggests that programme management is about doing the right work to achieve the high-level benefits, rather than just focusing on the projects within the programme delivering their outputs in line with agreed time, cost and quality objectives. As a result, programme managers are intended to focus on facilitating and leading change, leaving the work of project management to the project managers within the programme. Often the programme manager will take the role of the sponsor for the projects within the programme.

Programme management is needed to make sure that the right projects and other work is chosen so that the organisation achieves the strategic benefits. It provides clear linkage between projects and business goals so work is not wasteful and attention is not diverted to work that is not essential. It also manages the interfaces between projects and maintains a clear focus on the future benefits. The projects within the programme concentrate on delivering their specific outputs.

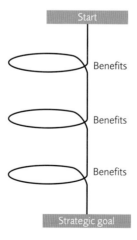

Figure 2.1 Programme spiral life cycle

Project Children's Hospice (PCH)

The project that you are managing is part of the Children's Hospice charity's annual fundraising campaign, or annual programme. The aim of this year's campaign, like all others, is to raise a significant amount of money for the causes that it supports. Projects like yours form a key part of this programme, along with other projects such as creating and selling a calendar and Christmas cards. The programme manager for the Children's Hospice is always looking for other good ideas to assist in achieving the strategic objective of raising lots of money. It is likely that a number of new projects will be added to the programme and, depending on their contribution to the financial target, these may well replace existing projects that have already been started.

What is a portfolio and what is portfolio management?

A portfolio is a grouping or bundle of projects and/or programmes collected together for management convenience under the sponsorship of an organisation, or a specific part of an organisation.

Portfolios of projects are often only related by the use of common **resources**, such as people or money. An example of a portfolio of projects would be all the work taking place in a company's IT department during the next financial year. Although some of the projects may share the same strategic objective, many of them are unrelated other than that they share resources and are taking place within the same time frame. Another example would be all the projects being undertaken by a railway maintenance contractor working in one regional area. Many of the projects that make up this portfolio will be geographically separated but will still use the same resources.

Portfolios of programmes are related because they represent the collection of work being carried out by a whole organisation or significant sub-set of an organisation. An example of a portfolio of programmes would be all the change-related work taking place within a government department such as the Department for Education.

Where programmes are said to have a common goal, portfolios of projects and portfolios of programmes can both be said to have a common theme.

Portfolio management is the selection, prioritisation and management of groups of projects and other work at either functional (departmental) or

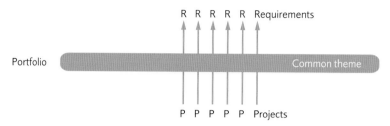

Figure 2.2 A portfolio

organisational levels, taking into account resource constraints. Because a portfolio has a common theme and not a common goal as in the case of a programme, the priorities for management are different. This can be especially important when the resource constraint relates to money or the funds available for capital investment.

The most important concept here is that the management of a portfolio gives an organisation a **method** to manage resource constraints by making sure that precious and scarce resources are used in the most efficient way possible. This can only be done if priorities can be defined between projects (or programmes) in a portfolio. Setting priorities and making tough decisions about how resources will be used is therefore the most essential aspect of portfolio management.

Project Children's Hospice (PCH)

Although you have accepted the role of project manager for PCH, you also have a number of other projects and routine jobs to do. Within the next three months you need to prepare a detailed presentation on how the company can improve its project management processes for the business change steering committee. You also want to find somewhere else to live, as you are unhappy in your rented flat, and you want to research and book a holiday.

If delivering the PCH project, presenting project management improvements, finding somewhere else to live and your holiday are considered as four projects, then what you are managing overall is a portfolio. The projects in this portfolio are linked together by two aspects: first, they are taking place in the same time frame and second, they share a common resource – you. They do not have a common goal but they have a common theme. Thinking of the four projects as a group (portfolio), alongside your usual daily tasks, will help you to plan and manage your time most efficiently.

3

Organising for projects

In Chapter 1 we discussed the differences between projects and business-as-usual. The fact that the two differ means that the way in which a business is organised to deliver projects is often different from the way on-going operations are organised.

The different roles and responsibilities required in the management of projects

There are five primary roles that are required in order to effectively manage a project. These are:

- The sponsor (sometimes called project executive) is the individual for whom the project is undertaken and is the primary risk taker. The sponsor owns the **business case** – the document that justifies the investment in the project – and is ultimately accountable to the senior management of the organisation who are investing for a desired outcome to be achieved. The term **sponsorship** is used to describe what a sponsor effectively does, see below. The responsibility of the sponsor is to ensure that the project remains a viable proposition and that benefits are realised. The sponsor must resolve or help to resolve any **issues** outside the control of the project manager.
- The project manager is the individual with the day-to-day responsibility and authority for delivering the project in line with specific objectives, including those relating to time, cost and quality. The project manager owns the **project management plan (PMP)** and is accountable to the sponsor for the effective implementation of that plan.
- The **user** or senior user represents the people who are intended to use the project outputs for the benefit of the organisation. **Users** are often referred to as 'the business'. One responsibility of the user is to define **acceptance criteria**, i.e. the requirements and essential conditions that have to be achieved before project outputs will be accepted.
- The project **team member** is allocated work to perform on the project and is responsible to the project manager for that work, irrespective of their 'normal'

19

reporting line outside of the project. Project team members can be staff of the organisation, **suppliers**, contractors, consultants, or in some rarer cases, members of the customer's organisation. Project team members may be more junior or more senior than the project manager, but for that project they must take direction from him or her.

- The steering group (sometimes called steering committee or project board) represents the senior management of the organisation that is investing in the project. The senior user will be a member of the project steering group, along with senior functional (departmental) managers who provide resources for the project and other representatives of key stakeholders. The senior functional managers are sometimes called senior suppliers. The sponsor is chosen by and is accountable to the project steering group and also typically chairs the meetings of the group. The project steering group must provide both strategic direction and guidance to the sponsor, and clarity of purpose for the project manager and their project team members.

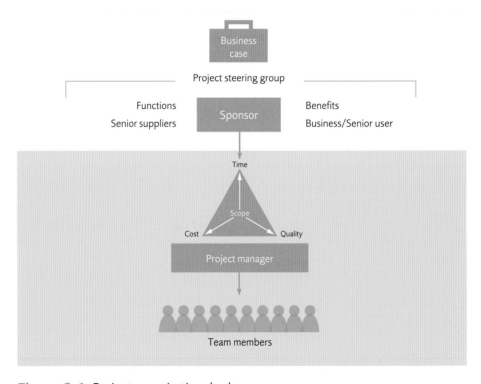

Figure 3.1 Project organisational roles

The first three of these roles – sponsor, project manager and user – are essential to all projects. Sometimes a project manager may be asked to also take on the responsibilities of the sponsor and/or user as well as their own; this is not effective. Only if each role is fulfilled by different people can the internal contradictions and conflicting requirements of the project be effectively managed.

Governance and sponsorship of projects

It is essential that all the projects undertaken by a business are carried out in a manner that does not jeopardise the on-going viability of that business. **Governance** sets out the policies, regulations, functions, methods, processes, **procedures** and responsibilities that should be used to manage and control a project (or programme or portfolio). Sponsorship (carried out by the sponsor) ensures that appropriate governance is applied and that the project delivers the benefits desired by the business.

Organisations that have inadequate governance and sponsorship often find themselves attempting to deliver projects that have no justifiable business need or have the ability to severely damage the integrity of the organisation itself.

The project management office

Many organisations use a specialised function to assist in the planning and monitoring of project delivery. This function can have different names. The most commonly used name is Project Management Office or PMO. This can be shortened to just **Project Office**. In some industries this function is known as Project Services or Project Controls.

The role of the PMO is to provide project management support in the form of information and specialist advice primarily relating to the project's schedule and budget/**estimate**. In many instances, a project's PMO will also be responsible for the administration of key project management processes and procedures including **risk management**, **change control** and **issue management**. Some PMOs also take responsibility for document management and an element of quality control. A PMO manager will head-up the PMO and will be a key supporting role for the project manager.

The acronym PMO can also be used (often confusingly) for a Programme Management Office, or a Portfolio Management Office. In these scenarios, the

PMO is supporting the objectives of a single programme, or of an overarching, 'enterprise wide' portfolio. PMOs that support more than one project often take on responsibility for the governance of all projects on behalf of the organisation.

Methods, processes and procedures

A method embodies the practices that are seen as 'best' for the organisation at that time. Methods provide consistent guidelines for people involved in projects, programmes and portfolios. Some organisations use their own bespoke approach, while others use approaches that are publicly available, such as PRINCE2®. Methods to be used will be determined by the project's governance. The PMO will often oversee the correct application of the chosen method.

Procedures describe the sequential steps that need to be followed in order to perform project management processes such as risk management and change control. The processes and procedures that will be followed on a project are documented in the project management plan (PMP).

Project Children's Hospice (PCH)

The key roles for the project have been identified. You are the project manager and your boss is the sponsor. You and the sponsor have decided that the 'user' representative should be a member who is not part of the organising group. Team members include the health and safety officer, the security adviser, the event managers, the finance manager and the quality manager. You will hold a meeting of all these people to discuss the project management plan (PMP) and to ask them to agree and sign-off the content.

You haven't decided if you need a steering group but if you do it will include your boss as sponsor, the user (staff representative) and probably the managing director as he is a key stakeholder and is the sort of character who will want to be involved.

Organisation structures

In order to deliver projects, an organisation can structure itself in a number of ways depending on the characteristics of the projects being undertaken. There are basically three recognised organisational structures for the delivery of

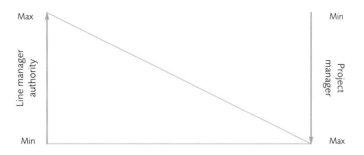

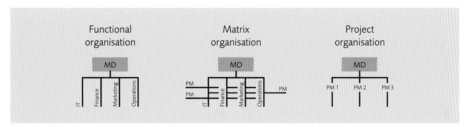

Figure 3.2 Organisation structures

projects: functional, matrix and project. These are often illustrated using a simple diagram (see Figure 3.2). In this diagram the **functional organisation** is on the left, the matrix in the middle and the project organisation is on the right. The significance of the line manager and project manager authority will be discussed below as part of the description of each organisation type.

Functional organisation

This is the traditional structure for most manufacturing-type companies where there is usually no separate project function or organisation. The function (sometimes called 'the line') utilises the natural business hierarchy where the emphasis is on operational procedures and business-as-usual to deliver projects. A functional/hierarchical organisation can have an adverse effect on project delivery. This is principally due to two factors:

- Delegated authority is strongest at the top of the hierarchy and reduces significantly as the level reduces.
- The cross-functional **communication** and cooperation that is vital for project management to be successful reduces as the height of the hierarchy increases.

This means that, unless the project manager holds a senior position in the hierarchy, the best they can do is coordinate the project, rather than manage it. Today this type of organisation is rarely used largely due to the increasing importance of project delivery to an organisation's success.

Project organisation

This is sometimes referred to as the purest project form of company organisation. For organisations whose normal business is projects (for example, contracting and consultancy companies), this structure is often a natural choice. In a **project organisation structure**, the project team is organised and remains as a multi-functional unit and, on project completion, is either disbanded or reformed and moved to another project. This organisational style is also referred to as a task force. Only very large or strategically important projects tend to use this type of structure as it also has its own problems:

- The potential disruption caused to business-as-usual when creating the organisation.
- What to do with those who are part of the project organisation once the project is over, especially if there are no more projects to work on.

It does have many good features, however, for example:

- It enables focused team working that is not distracted by anything else that is happening in the business.
- All necessary resources are dedicated to the project, therefore there are no delays while waiting for required expertise.

Matrix organisation

For organisations that recognise that projects are a **part** of its business – not a one-off or an unusual occurrence that might justify a functional structure, and not the major part of the business so justifying a project structure – the **matrix organisation structure** becomes the most relevant. In a matrix structure people retain their function or line identity but add a project identity as well. This usually manifests itself as working part time in the function/line and part time in the project. The balance between the 'day-job' and the 'project' is unlikely to be constant and will depend on the relative demands of the two roles.

This organisational style is often considered the compromise solution as it tries to bridge between pure project and functional styles. This type of organisation has some complications:

- Individuals working in the matrix will appear to have at least two bosses.
- There will be a tension between line managers and project managers when it comes to giving instructions to individuals and expectation of performance.

It does, however, have some good features, for example:

- It permits on-going business-as-usual to continue while projects are being delivered.
- Functional expertise is maintained because individuals still maintain a relationship with their functional manager.

There is no single correct answer to the challenge of how to organise resources for projects. Organisations make compromises knowing the pros and cons of the choices they have made.

4

Project life cycles

The idea of the life cycle is one of the things that makes project work different from business-as-usual. You could say that all projects have a start, middle and end, whereas business-as-usual has only a middle. The labels used to describe the phases of a life cycle are not usually as simple as start, middle and end. There are many different labels given to the phases within a life cycle depending on where you work and the history of the organisation. The key thing is to understand the purpose of the life cycle phases and not to worry about the different terminology used. You only need to understand the terms used in the organisation(s) you work within.

The project life cycle and project life cycle phases

Using a life cycle allows a project to be considered as a sequence of phases that provide the structure and approach for delivering one distinct chunk of work at a time and ensuring that nothing has been missed.

Many life cycles are depicted as a downward staircase, typically called a **waterfall**. Sometimes life cycles are depicted as a straight line, a 'V' or a spiral, but these are less commonly used.

APM uses these four phases in this sequence:

Concept
      Definition
            Development
                  Handover and closure

It is not unusual for organisations to use different terms for life cycle phases, e.g. **concept** is sometimes called initiation, **definition** is sometimes called planning and **development** is often called delivery, implementation or execution.

You will see from these words that the labelling of life cycle phases is a potentially confusing area when starting out in project management; the main thing to understand is the reason for splitting projects into life cycle phases as a way of controlling the project as effectively as possible.

> **Project Children's Hospice (PCH)**
>
> You have decided that your project to raise money for the charity is made up of four distinct phases – aligned to the terms used by APM. Figure 4.1 illustrates the life cycle of the project.
>
> Mapping the project life cycle to the APM life cycle above means that the pre-authorisation and consultation with staff are part of 'concept'. Designing and planning for the event is part of 'definition'. Communication and the day itself are part of 'development', and collecting donations as well as the **post-project review** is part of **'handover and closure'**.

The reasons for splitting projects into phases

All projects should be managed using a life cycle for the following reasons:

- The life cycle divides the project into manageable pieces or phases (sometimes loosely referred to as 'chunks').
- It ensures that the early phases of a project are not ignored.
- Treating each phase of the project as a mini-project will ensure that each phase is itself started correctly, planned, monitored and closed with lessons learned for the future.
- It assists in project planning and, in particular, in scheduling and estimating.
- Resources can be allocated to each phase and, as a result, resource shortages or clashes across projects can be predicted.
- It provides a mechanism to review what has actually happened compared to the plan and to make sure that the business case is still valid.
- It provides a means of reporting project status using a consistent set of terms and phase descriptions.
- It encourages interim project reviews at the end of each phase.
- It facilitates formal 'go/no go' decision making at the end of each phase.

The last bullet point is particularly important. It means that a project will never be able to pass from being just 'a good idea' to a completed product without a

Phase name	Duration	Week 1	Week 2	Week 3	Week 4	Week 5	Week 6	Week 7	Week 8	Week 9	Week 10	Week 11	Week 12	Week 13	Week 14	Week 15
Concept																
Pre-authorisation	4 days															
Consult with staff	15 days															
Definition																
Design & plan events	25 days															
Development																
Communicate	6 days															
Prep/the day	9 days															
Handover & closure	2 days															
Collect donations	96 days															
Present funds & PPR	5 days															

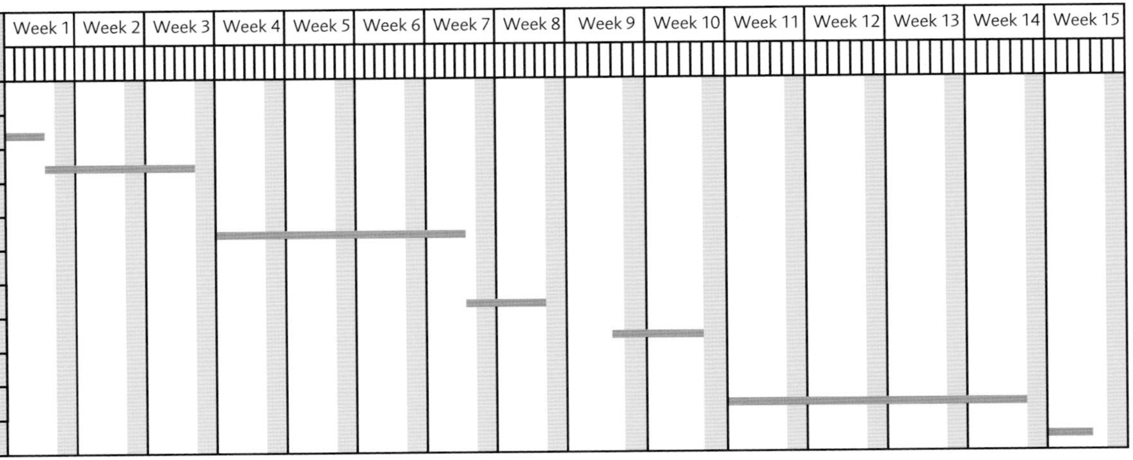

Figure 4.1 Project Children's Hospital (PCH) life cycle

number of checks and balances. Typical phase review points or **gates** (see below) might take place after:

- production of the initial business case
- production of the project management plan (PMP)
- completion of design
- completion of delivery prior to commissioning and use.

Or they might take place before:

- awarding of major contracts
- starting major build works (for IT or construction)
- starting a major roll-out following a pilot.

At each go/no-go decision point, the current project status or health should be compared to the current approved business case. This will itself help in the review and approval process. It is the sponsor's role to ensure that the appropriate level of approval is gained to proceed to the next project phase, assuming that they cannot give approval themselves.

Effective implementation of the go/no-go decision points will ensure that only those projects that should go ahead actually do so and those that should be cancelled are actually stopped. This means in turn that more projects will be successful in delivering the benefits they set out to achieve.

Formal gate reviews

It is now common practice to refer to the end of a phase within the project life cycle as a 'gate' or 'gateway'. Each gate is a defined decision point where senior stakeholders can decide whether to continue with the next phase as planned, to change plans or cancel the project. The **gate review** is the process that the decision makers go through at each gate. Each gate review should be informed by progress to date, future plans and a review of the current circumstances. Results from project audits or from **project evaluation reviews** during the phase in question may inform a gate review.

Organisations that manage this process well are confident that they work only on projects that are going to deliver the desired **success criteria** and benefits. This is not only useful to the sponsor and other senior managers who are making the investment decisions, but also for the project manager and project team, as

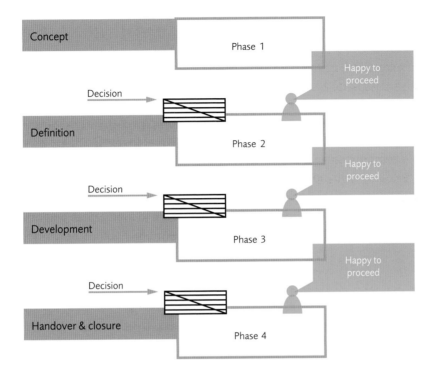

Figure 4.2 Gate reviews provide confidence

they know they are always doing work that is valued. Effective gate reviews stop projects that no longer meet the organisation's needs.

Project Children's Hospice (PCH)

Considering the life cycle as shown in Figure 4.1, phase review points or project gate reviews should take place after:

- staff consultation is complete
- event design and project management plan are agreed
- PCH day is complete
- sponsorship money is collected.

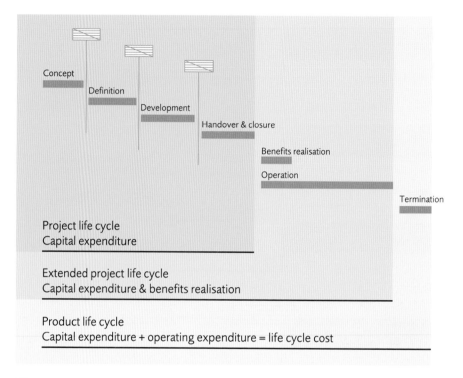

Figure 4.3 Extended and product life cycles

Other types of life cycle

In addition to the typical project life cycle there are two other variants that are worth considering as illustrated in Figure 4.3.

Extended life cycle: Recognises the operational phase of the project during which **realisation** takes place. The emphasis on benefits realisation is made to ensure that the agreed benefits are derived from the outputs and outcomes of the project. Often the responsibility for operations and benefits realisation falls outside the project delivery organisation's scope and influence.

Product life cycle: A further refinement of the extended life cycle that includes the final act of decommissioning/disposal of a product or service at the end of Termination phase. It is important to recognise the product life cycle when considering the total cost of ownership (TCO) or **life cycle cost** of the project.

In some instances, for example in nuclear decommissioning, it can be more expensive to terminate a project than it cost to create the project in the first place.

Waterfall versus agile

All of the three life cycles described above can be considered as 'waterfall' or linear life cycles, i.e. one project phase follows another. An alternative method for delivering certain types of projects is to utilise an approach known as **agile**. Using an agile approach, requirements and solutions are developed iteratively and incrementally throughout the project. Agile does not supersede the complete project life cycle, as a business case still needs to be created and benefits realised, but during the more traditional definition/planning and development/delivery phases, the agile approach adopts short cycles of 'doing, sharing and approval' work moving on incrementally. This can introduce re-work that ordinarily would be seen as wasteful, but agile approaches have been demonstrated to facilitate speed and **stakeholder engagement**, specifically in software development where the approach was developed. Using an agile approach, project scope and quality is typically sacrificed to hold time and cost objectives.

Although the title of this section is *waterfall* vs. *agile*, and many project management commentators offer an agile approach as an *alternative* to a traditional waterfall-based life cycle, it is most useful to think about how agile methods can be incorporated into the overall project life cycle for the benefit of overall project success.

5

Teamwork and leadership

In some ways, the ideas behind teamwork and **leadership** are the same in all situations where people are involved because any work requires groups of people to be motivated to do that work in the best possible way. Many argue, though, that managing people in a project context requires even more of a focus on teamwork and leadership than in a business-as-usual situation. This is because there is additional stress in situations when a temporary, multi-disciplinary team is brought together for a limited time to achieve objectives within time, cost and quality constraints. In such situations the project manager may not always have direct authority over team members and therefore must often lead through influence rather than direct line responsibility.

Project team, teamwork, team building and team development

The project team is the set of individuals (groups or organisations) that is responsible to the project manager for undertaking project activities. What links them together is that they are all working together to meet a common objective, i.e. to deliver the project to its time, cost and quality criteria. When people are working collaboratively towards a common goal this is called teamwork and is a particularly cohesive and effective form of group working.

Teams are always made up of a group of people with different technical and functional expertise. The effectiveness of the team will have a dramatic effect on the performance of the project. The most effective teams are not made up of people who have exactly the same outlook on life, the same preferences or the same habits. Bringing together a selection of people with different ideas and 'styles' will help the team to perform most effectively.

In the 1970s and 1980s it was very common for the entire project team to be co-located – literally in one office. Today this is becoming far less common, with the result that the virtual team, i.e. a team that doesn't usually meet face-to-face and is geographically dispersed, is becoming far more common. Managing a

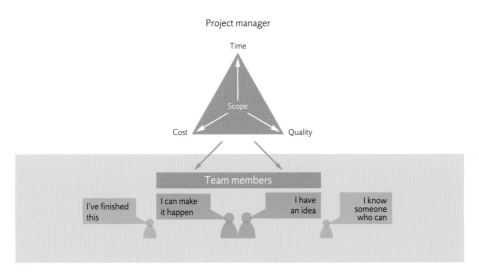

Figure 5.1 The project team

virtual team brings new challenges to project management, particularly when the team has never, and is unlikely to ever, meet face-to-face.

The challenge for the project manager is how to bring together a group of people and help them to bond and to work together as an effective and developing team focused on achieving the project success criteria and associated benefits. This is difficult enough when the project manager is able to choose their team, but in the majority of circumstances this is not possible; team members are 'allocated' to the project and the project manager works with whomever they have available.

As a project manager, therefore, perhaps the most important task is to continually reflect on how to communicate with the team, getting to know people well enough to understand what is needed to motivate them and deciding how best to inspire both individuals and the collective unit to do their best work, even when the project is difficult. To do this the project may need to encourage or organise team-building events, if there is a budget available; if it is possible, then such things as formal project launch/kick-off meetings, team 'away days' or planned social activities can be very beneficial.

Leadership and the role of the leader

A group of people thrown together to form a project team is unlikely to work well together from the outset. They are likely to need some support with team building and development from someone in a leadership role. Within a project, the project manager is expected to take the role of the leader. It is also very useful if the project sponsor has well-developed leadership capabilities.

Leadership is the ability to establish vision and direction, to influence and align others towards a common purpose and to empower and inspire people to achieve project success. It enables the project to proceed in an environment of change and uncertainty.

For the team to start to perform in an effective manner it needs to be recognised that it will pass through a number of development stages. These stages are often known as forming (initial coming together), storming (jostling for position and to understand roles and contributions), norming (agreement on roles and contributions) and performing (carrying out the agreed roles and contributions). The names for the stages of **team development** outlined above were developed by Bruce Tuckman in the 1960s (the **Tuckman team-development model**). Tuckman's research found that teams develop in maturity and ability as relationships are established. He also noticed that effective team leaders are able to flex their style of management to match the situation and the maturity of the individuals within the team. Some situations warrant a directive style, for example, if there is an emergency. In normal situations, most people respond best to a style where they are either coached by the leader or are given more autonomy to make decisions, but with the safety net of the leader in close proximity. With experienced team members, the project manager may be able to delegate significant parts of the work with full confidence, but it is also vital that relationships are such that the project manager knows whether the current leadership style they are adopting is working or not. It is a continual process of growing and learning together.

Unfortunately, some teams never make it to the performing stage; instead, they spend their time forming and storming and, as a result, work very inefficiently and ineffectively. Project managers should take responsibility for helping the team to move quickly and effectively through the development stages, for example by communicating the vision and providing clear objectives, roles and responsibilities at the start, or by being willing to adopt a style that trusts the team members to decide how to perform activities as they become more mature. As leaders need to be able to adopt different styles and approaches at different times, and they need

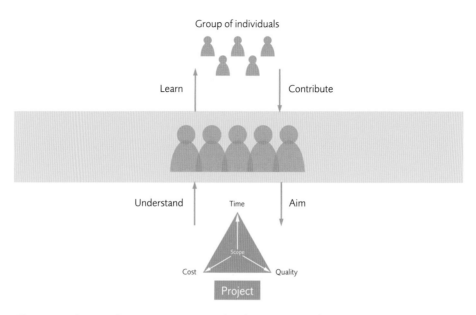

Figure 5.2 Good project managers lead groups into becoming a team

to choose the most appropriate style and approach for the situation, it is often said that the project manager should display **situational leadership**.

Figure 5.2 makes it clear that for a group to perform as a team there needs to be a focus on objectives and also processes in place whereby individuals can learn and grow as a result of their experience. It is the leader's role to facilitate the transition from group to team. The leader of any project has a direct and significant impact on team performance.

The subject of leadership cannot be covered in depth in this book and there are many different views on the attributes and qualities of a good leader. There is agreement, however, that effective leaders demonstrate a willingness and ability to:

- communicate a vision and inspire the team to align to achieve the vision
- listen to different views and to find a way forward that the majority of stakeholders can understand and respect, even if it's not their personal chosen path
- make decisions, weighing the benefits, costs and risks associated with the decision
- give and receive feedback in the interests of building a high-performing team.

Teamwork and leadership are easy to explain in theory, but difficult to get right in practice. When it's working on your project, you'll know it.

Project Children's Hospice (PCH)

Although you have not been able to select all of your team members, you have been able to select three 'games' managers to manage specific games on the day. In selecting the three games managers you have been proactive in making sure that you have chosen three different characters:

- Game manager 1 is full of ideas and always comes up with solutions to difficult problems.
- Game manager 2 is good at ensuring that things get done as well as being an effective team-worker.
- Game manager 3 has a lot of contacts with the company and is very reliable.

You are a pedant with an eye for detail and will be keen to monitor that things are going to plan. You firmly believe that the mix of people you have been able to put together will help you succeed in delivering the project, but you know that you will also need to take some actions to lead the team and help them work collaboratively towards the objectives.

In order to overcome any initial team development problems, you have arranged for a formal project launch meeting to take place. The meeting will be attended by the:

- sponsor
- health and safety officer
- security adviser
- three games managers
- finance manager
- quality manager.

At this meeting you will confirm everyone's roles and responsibilities as well as the project's objectives and you will try your best to build enthusiasm for the vision. After that you are hoping that the team will work well together and that there will be very little conflict, although you know that you will need to monitor this closely, as any problems will affect your ability to deliver the project objectives. If conflicts do arise, you know that it will be your responsibility to intervene and try to find a resolution that protects relationships as well as the project objectives.

You have already spoken to each of the people involved, so you are hoping that there will be no surprises – but you can never be sure.

6

Conflict management and negotiation

As we have already said, project teams are temporary organisations made up of people from different parts of your organisation and from other parties, such as suppliers and sometimes customers. Project teams are rarely located in the same office, and even if they are, the process of project working can often cause conflict. It is important, therefore, that the project manager has some understanding of **conflict management** and some approaches they have practised to help team members get the best outcome from conflict situations.

What is conflict management?

On first consideration you could be forgiven for thinking that conflict is bad – destructive and to be avoided. In this regard the word conflict is similar to the word 'risk' in our normal vocabulary. But just as in projects we think of risk as 'uncertainty that matters' – either positive opportunity or negative threat – so too with conflict there are positive as well as negative effects of differences in opinion, perspective, values etc.

Conflict, therefore, is the difference in objectives and attitudes between two or more parties. Conflict management is the process of identifying and addressing such differences that, if left unresolved, could affect project objectives.

Examples of how conflict arises in a project include:

- achievability of the schedule and allocated budget
- differences in opinions over requirements (what should be included or not)
- agreement of performance specifications
- competition for, or availability of, resources, including money
- individual roles and responsibilities
- fitness for purpose of **deliverables**.

41

How can the project manager manage conflict?

The points made in the teamwork and leadership chapter clearly apply. If the project manager does not have a knowledge of team members sufficient to provide clues about their behaviour, both when relaxed and when under pressure, it is difficult to know whether a short outburst under pressure is symptomatic of a wider negative conflict or not. Similarly, not everyone who has a difference of opinion or attitude with another person will express this, so it's important to be close enough to know what is going on in the team. Maybe there will be an opportunity for a creative solution to a difference between two team members. Most innovation comes out of difference, not similarity.

Thomas and Kilmann, two American researchers, have spent more than 30 years studying how people behave when faced with conflict. The 'Thomas-Kilmann **Conflict Mode Instrument**' suggests that there are five main ways to behave during conflict, based on two axes of 'concern for own point of view' and 'concern for other others' point of view', as shown in Figure 6.1.

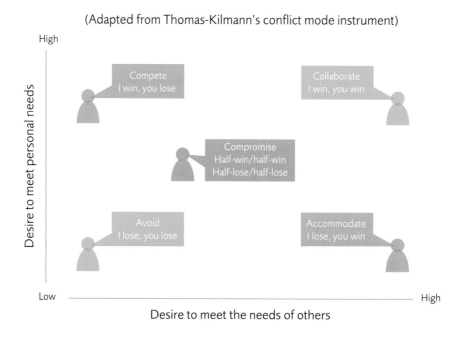

Figure 6.1 Ways of managing conflict

Another way of thinking about approaches to conflict management is to consider whether the approach creates a 'win-over' situation for either party or a 'win-win'. This is of particular interest when considering **negotiation** in project management.

Negotiation in project management

Negotiation is a discussion between two parties aimed at reaching an agreement. Negotiation skills are used in many areas of project management, such as conflict management, **procurement** and contract management, **requirements management** and stakeholder engagement. Negotiation is closely related to conflict management but tends to take a more structured approach, following a defined process (see Figure 6.2).

Preparation/Planning – Thorough preparation and planning for a negotiation is essential. This will include the development of an understanding of the other party's position. Other things, such as who will participate in the negotiation, its timing and location, need to be determined too.

Discussing – The start of a negotiation begins with discussion between those involved (the parties) with the express aim to create rapport, define the goal and establish a clear agenda.

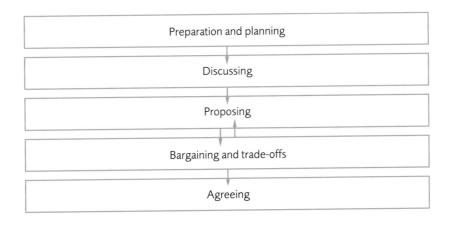

Figure 6.2 A five-stage negotiation process

Proposing – Usually one party will put their opening proposal on the table with an expectation of receiving counter-offers from the other parties.

Bargaining (and Trade-Offs) – This is often called 'give and take' – one party gains something by conceding something else. It is important when bargaining to ensure that there is room for negotiation, i.e. there is room to give something and/or concede something.

Agreeing – Having arrived at a final position (agreement), make sure it is documented and unambiguous. A **contract** is simply an agreement; if it has been signed, then there can be no valid argument as long as it is clear. Sadly many contracts associated with projects end up with lawyers and the courts involved, which suggests that this part of project management is not often done perfectly.

Negotiations can loosely be described as being *formal* or *informal*. **Formal** negotiations take place at pre-arranged meetings, often with external parties, such as when negotiating a legally binding contract. **Informal** negotiations can be seen as those that take place between project staff and other stakeholders. Often these are spontaneous and involve little or no pre-planning. As a result, the project manager needs to have well-developed negotiating skills to avoid coming to agreements that are not a win–win for the project and the people involved.

> ### Project Children's Hospice (PCH)
>
> You have already been faced with two conflict situations. The first occurred when one of the games managers (games manager 1) insisted that the fundraising event should be extended into the evening, as that would allow families to be involved, which they believed was fundamental to the success of the project. While you thought this was a good idea, you had already agreed with the sponsor and health and safety officer that this would not be the case, as it would complicate matters significantly. It was therefore important for the project that you resolved this conflict in a way that allowed you to win (and the event manager to back down, but remain committed to the project). Your second conflict arose when games manager 2's line manager told you that he was no longer available for the project. As games manager 2 had already started to develop some good ideas you were unhappy as you thought these would be lost. During amicable discussions

with the line manager you agreed that she would provide an alternative person and also allow time for a proper handover (win–win).

You had hoped that there wouldn't be a need to apply any formal **negotiation process** on this project. However, when you approached the local daily newspaper with a request to report on the event, rather than agreeing immediately, the editor asked you to pay a visit to their offices to discuss what might be done. Prior to visiting the newspapers offices you agreed with the sponsor what sort of coverage you would ideally like and that you would be the only one to attend the meeting from your side. Following some quick research, you found out that the newspaper was covering two other non-related events that day.

When you arrived at the editor's office things started off very amicably but it soon became clear that the PCH event was considered to be a lower priority than the other two events that were taking place that day. You made it clear that it was very important for this event, and your company, that decent, high-profile media coverage was achieved.

The editor's initial proposal was just to accept some photos taken by 'someone' at the event along with copy from you, and then use this to create a quarter page in an edition following soon after the event. You suggested that this was not suitable for an event related to such a good cause and a two-page spread would be more appropriate, and that they should send their own reporter and photographer. You also thought it would be a good idea if they did a small feature prior to the event to say what was going to happen (you could provide the copy for this).

The difference between the two starting positions inevitably led to some bargaining. Eventually you proposed that if the newspaper provided the coverage required, you would ensure that all internal publicity for the event included their logo in a prominent position. The newspaper finally agreed to give a you a quarter page prior to the event – with copy provided by you – and a one-page 'spread' of the event using their own reporter and photographer; this would be in the next day's edition. In turn, you agreed to include their logo on internal publicity materials and to give out free copies of the newspaper in your offices on the day of the event.

When you got back to the office you thought it would be wise to confirm these agreements in an email to the editor.

The concept (idea) phase

Introduction

In this section we look at the first phase on the project life cycle; the Concept phase. It is during this phase that the reason for doing the project (need, opportunity or problem) is confirmed, initial requirements identified, and the overall feasibility of the project is considered. In the Concept phase a number of tools, techniques and processes must be undertaken or carried out. Many of these approaches are continued in later life cycle phases, but it is vital they are started here.

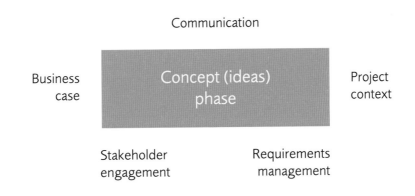

Figure 7.1 Concept (ideas) phase – overview

The objective of the Concept (ideas) phase is to agree the business case for the project, and to be able to do this so that the sponsor – the primary risk taker on the project – is satisfied that further investment in the project is justified. For this reason, no project should proceed into its later life cycle without an agreed business case.

7

Project context

You could say that the project **context** is the world in which the project is being carried out. As we live in an ever changing world we must be continually aware of what is going on around us.

The key point here is that understanding the project context (sometimes called project **environment**) helps with all aspects of project planning and management, specifically those related to stakeholder engagement, communication, **quality management** and risk management. It is important to understand two dimensions of context: first, the context that is internal to the company or organisation carrying out the project, e.g. the organisational sensitivity of the project; second, the context that is external to the project or organisation, i.e. the environment into which the project will be delivered.

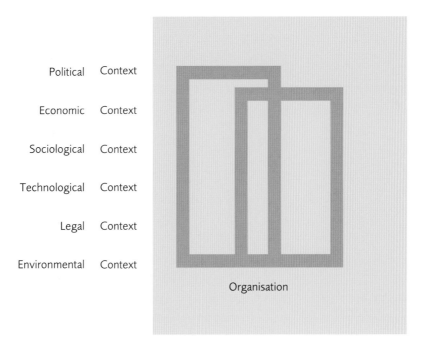

Political	Context
Economic	Context
Sociological	Context
Technological	Context
Legal	Context
Environmental	Context

Organisation

Figure 7.2 Understanding project context

There are a number of tools and techniques that can be used to understand the internal and external environment or project context. What they all have in common is a focus on the things that matter to stakeholders.

Different stakeholders care about different issues, such as finances or economic matters, technical or technology-based problems, or concerns about social or political situations. Others may care about the legality or environmental 'friendliness' of the project. If the project manager does not understand the project context, then they are attempting to achieve project objectives in a dangerous vacuum.

If a project manager fails to consider the context, the uncertainty leaves the project exposed to an increased level of risk, i.e. the chance that unidentified situations will impact on project objectives. The risks may be managed successfully (or the organisation might be lucky and get away with not managing a situation), but in practice it is safe to say that projects that are not grounded in a good under-standing of the wider context tend to run into significant problems and fail to deliver what is needed, on time or to budget. Ignoring reality doesn't work.

PESTLE analysis

Often the acronym **PESTLE** is used as a prompt list in analysing and under-standing the context of a project, and it provides a usable and effective structure for thinking about the wider environment into which the project must deliver. The acronym stands for:

- Political.
- Economic.
- Sociological.
- Technological.
- Legal.
- Environmental.

Consider the example of building a new tram system in a major city. **Politically**, the project may be seen as a 'pet project' for the current local authority, as it is part of an initiative to improve inner-city redevelopment. **Economically**, the project might be dependent on favourable private financing and will be linked to interest rates. **Socially**, the project will be seen as a means of removing cars from the city centre and hence improving public access and reducing journey times. If the project is being undertaken in a city centre that has narrow streets or is quite hilly, then from a **technical** perspective there might be some problems. The compulsory purchase of land or the disruption to business may mean that the project is **legally** challenged. Finally, such a project is almost certain to have **environmental** (ecological) aspects, as it will reduce pollution and noise levels during operation.

Project Children's Hospice (PCH)

Understanding the context in which you must deliver the project will help you in its management. Although most people in the company will be aware of the local children's hospice charity and will support it, there are likely to be a few who actively support other charities and will not appreciate being asked to support this one. You will need to be *politically* sensitive when addressing this. The amount of money that you raise will be affected by the *economic* situation at the time. If the event day falls just after everyone has been paid you might end up raising quite a lot more than expected.

You also want to ensure that the individual games you plan are *socially* acceptable and don't cause any embarrassment or injury. You don't see any *technical* issues with the project, but you are concerned with possible *legal* obligations, therefore you will be talking to the company lawyer in advance. You will certainly make sure that you have good insurance cover. None of the games that you are currently contemplating will have any major *environmental* aspects. You will make sure that any rubbish or waste is properly disposed of and you will think about this further as you proceed to put together your plans.

Legal requirements

Although mentioned as the 'L' in PESTLE, it is important to emphasise the need to comply with the law and hence the legal systems in which the project is being carried out. Of course, there could be multiple legal jurisdictions that apply to a project if different parts of the scope are being carried out in different countries. The areas that project managers typically need to be aware of include laws that relate to health and safety, physical, data and cyber security, environment, employment and contracts. Ignorance of the law is never a defence for non-compliance.

Sustainability

PESTLE does not make a direct reference to **sustainability** because sustainability cuts across all six aspects. At a high level, sustainability considers the ecological/environmental, economic and social dimensions of the project. In order to do this, it must also take into account any political, technical and/or legal aspects that might have an influence on achieving a sustainable solution.

There has been a focus in recent times on sustainable projects – what does this mean? It is partly about desired project outcomes, but also about how the project is carried out. There is an increasing recognition that using natural and human resources indiscriminately to achieve growth and financial profit without regard to the environmental or social cost, is no longer acceptable. A sustainable project can mean many things and manifest itself in many ways. It is the project manager's responsibility, in conjunction with their team, to ensure that, wherever possible; sustainability is taken into account. This might include the use of conference calls rather than face-to-face meetings, or the re-use of materials and other artefacts rather than buying or creating new ones.

Project Children's Hospice (PCH)

You have thought about sustainability and have made two key decisions. First, you will ensure that the event day is designed in such a way as to make it sustainable in the future, i.e. that the event can be repeated if desired. Second, you will ask around to see if anyone can provide any equipment from local organisations that can be returned after the event. This will relieve you of the need to make some purchases as well as the need for future storage.

8

Stakeholder engagement

It is widely accepted that understanding and engaging with stakeholders is highly important for successful project management and should not be overlooked. A project manager needs to make sure that all stakeholders are identified and, where required, actively engaged. Key stakeholders don't tend to go away, so ignoring them usually causes problems of some description for the project. It was usual some years ago to talk about stakeholders being managed, rather than engaged. The change to using the language of engagement reflects the recognition that some, if not all, stakeholders cannot just be told what to do.

Stakeholders

A stakeholder is a person (or group of people) who has a role to play, or is interested in or affected by the project in some way. In terms of project management, a stakeholder is often described as anyone (or any organisation) that can help or hinder the project.

Understanding stakeholders and their needs is a very important aspect of project management and one of the key duties of the project manager. If stakeholder needs and expectations are understood from the start, the project manager can then communicate with these people (or groups) in an appropriate way as the project progresses. Keeping stakeholders 'on-side' and supportive of the project is an essential skill. This skill is formally called 'stakeholder engagement'.

Stakeholder engagement

Some stakeholders may not be very interested in the project at the start, but are nevertheless influential – for example, a trade union or staff representative. Their influence may begin to affect the project if one of their members should become aggrieved. Other stakeholders may be interested in the project, but are not very influential. For example, a manager in a department that is not involved in the project might want to see how the change will be implemented so they can consider

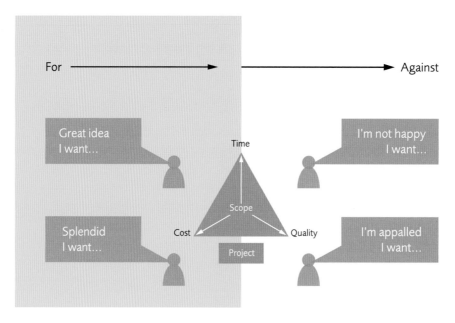

Figure 8.1 All stakeholders must be engaged

something similar in future. These stakeholders need to be engaged in addition to those who are both interested and influential from the start. Things change; when they do, the project manager needs to know who can help and who might hinder.

If understanding stakeholders is critical to effective project management, then it follows that stakeholder engagement should be a systematic part of the project manager's job. Engaging with stakeholders throughout the project life cycle is a key action to ensure that project communication works.

Project Children's Hospice (PCH)

There are a number of obvious stakeholders in this project. All those employed in the head office are stakeholders because you want to involve them in the activities on the day. Some of them are stakeholders in other ways. For example, your boss is a key stakeholder, as she has set out some constraints for the project that she will want you to adhere to, and she is the sponsor. The company's managing director is also a stakeholder, as he will not want anything to go wrong that might affect company performance or reputation in the local area. Company employees who have agreed to physically take part in organising and running the games you plan, and therefore might be a little concerned as to what they are letting themselves in for, are also stakeholders. You are a key stakeholder too. Other stakeholders will include those involved in the wider children's charity fundraising programme, although their interest is actually likely to be quite low. Knowing who the stakeholders are will enable you to engage them, e.g. if you want to put your participants' minds at ease you should let them know what you are thinking of doing and get their input as early as possible.

Stakeholder analysis

Because stakeholder identification and engagement is important, project managers and their team need to have ways of understanding what stake-holders think about the project. Most people do this using some form of **stakeholder analysis**.

One simple way of undertaking stakeholder analysis is for each identified stakeholder to consider three things. First, what their interest is in the project. Second, whether or not they can influence the project, and third, whether their attitude to the project is positive or negative. It is clear that those stakeholders who are very interested in the delivery of the forecasted benefits, and are influential enough to make the change happen, are very important, irrespective of whether their attitude is positive or negative. Their views need to be considered and any risks they identify, or issues they are aware of, should be explicitly addressed in the project management plan (PMP).

An example of such a group of interested and influential stakeholders might be the department affected by the introduction of new working practices. These will inevitably mean some job losses and will also mean new ways of working, using new systems and processes. Those who are remaining in the department will have to use the new systems and processes. If they are consulted during the preparation of the business case, they might identify risks such as 'key retained staff may not like the new ways of working and will leave of their own accord'. They also might identify issues such as 'staff are very concerned about the lack of information available and are also worried about job security'. The risks and issues identified should be considered when assessing the business case and when it is taken forward into the Definition phase of the project.

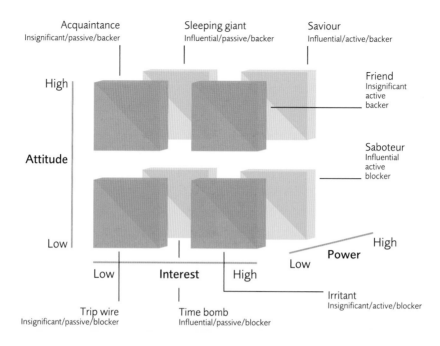

Figure 8.2 A stakeholder analysis tool (stakeholder cube)

In Figure 8.2 you can see one way of visualising a stakeholder's interest, influence and attitude towards the projects. This helps in performing an initial stakeholder analysis. The names assigned to each stakeholder are used to give a 'tongue-in-cheek' and over-arching perspective of each stakeholder type. They shouldn't be used to describe real people, of course.

Project Children's Hospice (PCH)

As you have already identified, there are a number of key or important stakeholders in the project, including you, the sponsor, team members and event participants. No in-depth stakeholder analysis has been carried out so far, so you know you need to do this and you think a good time would be as part of the staff consultation phase of the project life cycle. If any significant points arise, they can be fed into the business case and PMP. It would have been good to do this work earlier, but it is better to think about stakeholders later than not at all.

9

Requirements management

Requirements are the basis for any project; we carry out projects because 'someone' needs us to do something. Requirements describe what stakeholders (including customers and users) want and are used as the main input to the development of a solution and the way in which that solution is provided. If requirements are not adequately identified, specified and maintained, then substantial changes later in the project life cycle are inevitable – leading to cost increases, schedule overruns and dissatisfied stakeholders.

Requirements

Requirements are the clear and agreed expression of stakeholder's wants and needs with, importantly, a focus on what is necessary, not how it will be achieved. This may seem trivial but just to say 'I want the car go to fast' is clearly not enough. Frequently, when asked what they want, a stakeholder will ask for more than they actually need – 'I would like the car to be able to travel at 150 miles per hour'. Even though this happens, it is still wise to find out what people want before telling them they can't have it (or don't need it for a car that is to safely and legally commute to work every day).

Requirements management

Requirements management follows a simple process of capturing, analysing/ assessing and justifying stakeholders' perceived wants and needs, before baselining the agreement (see Figure 9.1). The importance of requirements management cannot be under-estimated if a successful project is to be delivered.

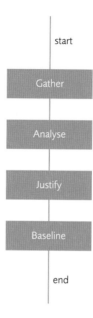

Figure 9.1 Requirements management

Gather

In this first step, requirements are obtained from all relevant sources. Requirements can be obtained from many sources including: stakeholders; the business case (if one exists at the point that requirements are captured); identified constraints; existing applications (similar projects); processes, standards and specifications. To be useful, requirements should be documented in such a way that they are comprehensive, clear, well structured, traceable and demonstrable through acceptance testing.

Note that acceptance tests are usually developed at the same time as the final requirements are agreed and can help clarify requirements and, in some cases, may lead to requirements being modified. Acceptance tests are best developed in conjunction with stakeholders. An acceptance test can be something as simple as switching a new device off and on 100 times, or something more complex like a driving a new car for 10 days across various terrains and in different weather conditions.

Analyse

During this step, requirements are analysed (assessed) with respect to other requirements, the project's context and the organisation, taking into consideration risks, benefits, business priorities and availability of resources, including the budget. Interdependencies between requirements are identified and documented to ensure that essential supporting requirements are not neglected. An example of this might be a requirement for ultra-fast hand-held wireless communications without having identified the need for the technical infrastructure to support it. Impact and feasibility studies are often undertaken to determine the likely effects of the requirements on the organisation and other stakeholders in terms, for example, of cost or future resource requirements. In addition, requirements are assessed to determine if they are obviously invalid, are incomplete, overlap or conflict with other requirements. Requirements are then amended, gathering additional information if necessary, to correct any deficiencies and to satisfy the criteria outlined above. The purpose of analysing requirements is to make sure nothing is missed.

Justify

In this step, all requirements must be prioritised and justified, taking care to distinguish wants from needs. Remember that when asked, most stakeholders *will* ask for more than they need.

One technique used to prioritise requirements is the **MoSCoW** approach, where:

- **M** represents the **must** haves for the solution to work and to deliver the main benefits.
- **S** represents the **should** haves that are desirable but not essential to benefits realisation.
- **C** represents the **could** haves that would be 'nice to have' as long as they don't affect anything else, i.e. they fit with the solution and can be delivered within the time and cost constraints.
- **W** represents the **won't** have this now, but may like it in the future if things change.

The prioritised requirements should be evaluated to ensure that they meet the project priorities and will deliver the benefits that are, or will be documented, in the business case. It is not unusual for stakeholders to hold competing or even conflicting requirements. In these instances, the project sponsor may need to intervene, negotiate and ultimately decide which stakeholder will be disappointed.

Baseline

This final step defines the **baseline** requirements of the entire set of needs that the project is expected to satisfy prior to commencing the next steps. All projects have time and cost constraints that will affect the extent to which requirements can be implemented within the project. Inevitably, some requirements gathered, analysed and justified earlier may still have to be excluded. The baseline requirements are **configuration** items, i.e. they are controlled so that any requests to change them are managed through the formal change control process. It is the baseline requirements that are used to develop the detailed scope for the project.

Project Children's Hospice (PCH)

You have decided that you will use the staff consultation phase to capture requirements from the team and also to analyse them (at least to some degree). For this type of project there is a clear need to justify the things that must happen from the 'nice to haves'. If any stakeholders have strong preferences about things that must or must not happen, it will be important to know. You are imagining that that people will think it's a 'must have' to have games where people don't get wet or dirty in the process – but you need to check this out and the other things that are important to take account of. You also need to be aware of any requirement from the charity itself, as well as any legal/insurance requirements (restrictions). Once you have all the requirements captured, analysed and justified you will document them and get them signed off by the sponsor (forming a baseline).

Requirements management through the project life cycle

Requirements will evolve during the Concept and Definition phases of the project. The requirements developed during the Concept phase will comprise a high-level view of the stakeholders wants and will not necessarily describe in full what is actually needed. As the project moves into the Definition phase, and more is known about possible solutions, the requirements will be revisited and refined to ensure that they remain realistic. During the Development phase the ultimate solution will be delivered and tested, the requirements forming the basis for acceptance tests before handover of the final project outputs to the business for use. Finally, during on-going operations, the project outputs will hopefully be seen to satisfy the agreed requirements and allow the business to deliver the desired outcomes and business benefits. Major changes to requirements must be managed through change control. This is described in Chapter 24.

10

Communication

Experienced project managers spend the vast majority of their time communicating in one form or another. It therefore follows that this is another foundational topic to consider when starting out in project management. It is also extremely important to consider all aspects of communication as early as possible in the project life cycle.

Communication and the contents of a communication plan

Communication is the transmission and receipt of information so that all parties receive and understand what the sender intends. Communication should never be a linear and one-way phenomenon. Others may interpret our words and actions differently from what was intended. It is also easy to assume similarity or difference when none exists. Effective communication is rarely about the simple confirmation of a message.

Figure 10.1 explains three general categories for methods of communication and suggests how 'rich' the communication is using each method. For example, a face-to-face encounter with someone means that the whole range of verbal and non-verbal clues are available to be interpreted, whereas a telephone call restricts the clues to those that can be heard, and a letter or report to only those clues that can be read. Choice of communication method and the media used is really important if you are to be sure that the recipient understands the message you are intending to send.

Email as a primary communication method is increasingly used, and perhaps over-used, in organisations. Everyone will have their own examples of where their intention in sending an email was misunderstood by the receiver. People now use email to be more than a 'words only' method, attempting to give other clues that reflect the emotion in the situation☺. Of course there are many other less official methods of communication ranging from instant messaging and

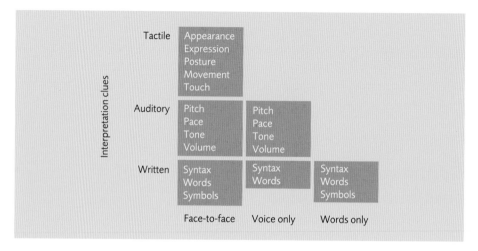

Figure 10.1 Methods of communication

'texts'/SMS through many different types of social media. All of these may have their place as part of a **communication plan**.

As there are many people to communicate with on a typical project, the project manager should prepare a communication plan. The communication plan typically contains details of what information is to be communicated, to whom, from whom, when and how often, where, how (through which medium), the desired impact, and perhaps why the communication is being made. It is the plan that describes how stakeholders will be practically engaged and influenced throughout the life of the project.

There are many different communication methods and media, each of which is useful in different situations. These include:

- impromptu one-to-one conversations – 'management by walking about'
- formal one-to-one meetings
- telephone conversations
- video conferencing
- email exchanges

- 'texts'/SMS
- written reports for formal presentation of selected information – different types of report may be required for different stakeholders
- progress meetings for communicating to a number of people simultaneously – however, to be most effective they need to be managed and have a proper agenda
- notice boards for communication of selected information
- newsletters for communication to a large group of stakeholders without any discrimination
- chat rooms on an intranet
- social media sites
- collaboration software
- road shows for communication to a more widely dispersed population of stakeholders.

The method used to communicate needs to be appropriate if the message and the meaning is to get through. For example, an appropriate method of giving feedback to a team member on performance issues would be on a one-to-one basis. An inappropriate method would be to mention it in a team meeting or via social media.

None of the above can be considered to be effective forms of communication without some sort of response from the recipient. It is therefore important that the project manager encourages feedback, and is available to receive responses and to listen to concerns through different communication channels.

Barriers to communication

When thinking about communication, and in particular developing a communication plan, it is important to consider some of the things that might make communication difficult. These are often said to be barriers to communication. These barriers are often subdivided into three types: psychological, technical and cultural.

Psychological barriers relate to the attitudes of those involved and the personalities of the sender and receiver of the communication. Factors like respect (or lack of) between those involved and whether or not the receiver likes or dislikes the sender are important here.

Technical barriers include the way the communication process is organised and structured. Things like the overuse of technical terms and jargon, abbre-

Methods	Frequency	From	To	Content & purpose
1:1	Weekly	PM	Sponsor	Progress reporting and issue management
1:1	Weekly	PM	Key stakeholders	Progress reporting
Phone	Daily	PM	Team members	Status updates
Email	Ad-hoc	PM	All stakeholders	Status updates
Meeting	Weekly	Team	Team	Progress reporting and corrective actions
Notice board	Continuous	PM	Head office staff	General communications and updates – money raised etc.
Newsletter	Monthly	Sponsor	Whole company	Awareness and fund raising

Figure 10.2 Communication plan for PCH

viations and acronyms and 'industry speak' can cause problems when communicating outside of the project.

Cultural barriers relate to the way we react to our own customs and local needs. These can be more difficult to appreciate as they include factors like religious belief and value systems (what is important to the receiver), as well as reflecting 'custom and practice' within a particular organisation.

Overcoming barriers to communication can take a lot of skill and appreciation of how people and organisations differ. Being aware that barriers exist is just the starting point. Skilled communicators will empathise with different needs and adjust their communication plans appropriately.

Project Children's Hospice (PCH)

Communication is going to prove a very important part of the project. If no one knows about the event that is going to take place, you'll raise very little money and the day will be a disaster.

You will prepare a communication plan for the project. You have already identified the following methods of communication that you will use:

- formal one-to-one meetings with the sponsor and other key stakeholders, such as the managing director on a weekly basis
- daily telephone conversations with team members
- email exchanges to keep some stakeholders up-to-date on an ad-hoc basis
- progress meetings for communicating to the whole project team – you intend to hold these on a weekly basis
- notice boards for communication of event information to all the staff in head office
- the company newsletter for communication to the whole company – you believe that this may allow you to raise more money.

11

Project success

Knowing what success looks like, and knowing you have achieved it, is fundamental to project management. What project success entails needs to be fully understood by all those involved in projects. A project is only truly successful if it delivers the specified requirements (outputs or deliverables) on time, within the agreed budget and to the agreed quality, such that the derived outcomes allow the promised benefits to be achieved. A project that delivers its outputs in line with time, cost and quality objectives but doesn't deliver the promised benefits is almost always a failure. Slightly controversially a project that delivers its promised benefits having been late, over budget and with a lower quality can often be considered successful. There are many examples of this, such as the Sydney Opera House, which was 10 years late and 14 times over budget but which has nevertheless been successful both as an architectural icon and a moneymaker for the city.

Outputs, outcomes and benefits

You have hopefully noticed that we have used the terms outputs, outcomes and benefits already a number of times in this book. There are official APM definitions for these terms, but other words also tend to be used interchangeably, as follows:

Outputs: Defined as the tangible or intangible products typically delivered by a project. You can use the term output, product and deliverable interchangeably. We will also expand on the idea of a project's products further in Chapter 13.

Outcomes: Defined as the changed circumstances or behaviour that results from the use of an output. Some projects deliver outputs and hand them over to the business for them to create the desired outcomes. Increasingly though projects have a high degree of business involvement to ensure not only that the project delivers outputs, but that the desired outcomes are assured. We expand on this idea later in this chapter.

Benefits: Defined as the quantifiable and measurable improvement resulting from outcomes perceived as positive by a stakeholder. More on this below.

Project success criteria and key performance indicators (KPIs)

Project success criteria are the criteria by which the success of a project will be judged in terms of delivering outputs. Without success criteria, any project that is actually completed could be argued to be a success, irrespective of whether it was delivered on time, to budget or to the agreed quality specifications.

The project's time, cost and quality objectives will inevitably form at least some of the project's success criteria. For example, for the project to be successful, it should:

- be complete by 31 December 2019
- cost no more than £500,000
- deliver products and services that meet specification X456.

Some projects warrant additional success criteria, e.g. all employees who remain with the company after the reorganisation are happy in their new job, or everybody who takes the examination passes.

While some people will differentiate between the terms *objective*, i.e. a predetermined result against which effort is directed and *success criteria*, i.e. the criteria against which success of the project may be judged for the purposes of this book, the terms are used interchangeably.

If success criteria are those aspects of the project that matter to stakeholders and will be used to judge whether the project was successful or not, then it makes sense that they need to be measured and monitored as the project progresses through the life cycle.

Project Children's Hospice (PCH)

You have agreed that the success criteria for the project are as follows:

- The project is a workplace event and should involve as many people as possible.
- It must take place in exactly 10 weeks' time, and all the money collected should be received or collected within four weeks of the close of the event.
- It must utilise no more than 1,000 hours of company time, and require no more than an additional £500 of company expenditure.

- It should aim to raise £10,000 for the children's hospice charity.
- There should be no complaints from staff about the event or the games that form part of it.
- There should be no complaints from customers about reduced service as a result of staff participation in the event.
- The company should get good press through local newspaper, radio and TV coverage.
- When questioned after the project has completed, 90% of staff would agree to do it again next year.

Key performance indicators (KPIs) can be defined as the measures that are indicative of whether or not the project is progressing towards a successful conclusion. KPIs are used to establish a measurement baseline at the start of a project so that progress can be monitored throughout and success judged at the end of the project. This is easy for tangible things, such as 'cost no more than £500,000', but it is more difficult for less tangible success criteria, such as 'employees are happy in their new job'.

It would be easy for the project to concentrate on things that are easy to measure and ignore the others, but this is a mistake. Creative ways of measuring those less tangible criteria that inevitably reflect on the success of the project need to be found, for example, by using creative ways of understanding employee satisfaction other than monitoring sickness absence or retention rates.

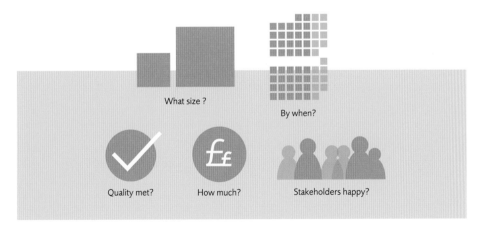

Figure 11.1 Success criteria

73

Project Children's Hospice (PCH)

It will be important to monitor progress towards the success criteria. Key performance indicators (KPIs) will include:

- the number of people actively taking part in the project on a day-to-day basis including the number of volunteers to participate on the day itself
- the amount of time being expended on the project as tracked by the company's time recording system
- the amount of money pledged to the charity as reported on a weekly basis
- the number of (or lack of) phone calls/emails received by HR from staff complaining about the event as logged in the staff complaints book
- interest from local media as measured by number of phone calls received.

Benefits

Use of the term benefit alongside success criteria within project management was once an unusual occurrence but is today commonplace. Some people argue that programmes deliver benefits and projects deliver outputs, which the programme then uses to create outcomes of benefit for the organisation. Where a project is part of a programme this is the case, but that doesn't mean that projects alone never deliver benefits. A starting out book is not the place to argue this further, but it is useful to be aware.

Project success criteria focus on the project – the things that the project manager has to deliver for his or her project to be successful. Benefits focus on the business – the things that the sponsor must achieve to be successful by taking the completed project deliverables (outputs), such as a new IT system, and through the use of that new system (outcome) realising benefit for the business.

Some benefits can be measured in monetary terms, such as reduced costs or increased revenues, and these are often used as the basis for the business case because they tangibly justify the financial investment in the project. Projects also deliver desired outcomes where cash proxies are difficult to establish so non-financial measures are used. Examples include benefits such as increasing safety, increasing employee satisfaction or increasing customer satisfaction. It is possible to put a monetary value to these but this should only be done where there is a method in place to measure the benefit and attribute the effect directly

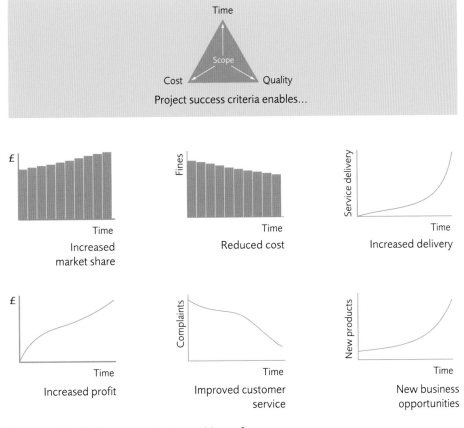

Figure 11.2 Success criteria and benefits

to the project. Whenever possible the description of a benefit should be 'SMART' (specific, measurable, achievable, realistic and time-bound). A benefit that just says 'increased profit' cannot be measured and is of little value when used as part of a business case.

Project Children's Hospice (PCH)

The benefits of the project are:

- raising money for a really important local cause
- increased staff morale as measured by the annual staff survey

- a higher ranking in the annual 'best place to work' report that will encourage good people to want to join the company
- an increased public awareness of the company and positive impact on the company's image leading, hopefully but not measurably within this project, to increased sales.

Success factors

For projects to achieve their success criteria and deliver their desired benefits it helps that a number of generic factors are in place. It is easy to spot when these factors are missing as the project tends to feel like it is not going well, but when they are in place things feel good. These 'feel good' factors, when present in the project environment, positively help the achievement of a successful project; they are formally called **success factors**. If success factors are absent then the project is more likely to fail. Some would say that there are a number of success factors that are more important than others. These are often called **critical success factors (CSF)** because if any of them are absent the project will fail in one way or another.

Numerous lists of critical success factors have been produced by people who research and write about project management. Common to most lists are the following:

- *clear goals and objectives*, without which there will not be any clear understanding of what the project is setting out to achieve and what its objectives are
- *good sponsorship or senior management support* for the project, without which the project will find itself struggling to get committed resources and organisational buy-in
- *open consultation and communication* with all those involved, i.e. all stakeholders
- *realistic plans* that can be followed and then used for monitoring and control
- *a motivated and competent project team* that will want to carry out the project and have the ability to deliver it.

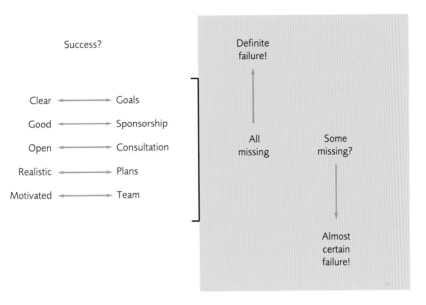

Figure 11.3 Critical success factors

Project Children's Hospice (PCH)

All of the critical success factors outlined above apply equally to the children's hospice project. It is clear that if senior management remove their support, it is quite likely that those needed to participate will find other things to do. Likewise, if you as project manager find that key stakeholders are unclear about what you are doing, you have failed to have open communication with them.

It is difficult to actually measure whether critical success factors are in place but, as mentioned above, it is easy to spot when they are not. If any of the following occur, it is likely that one or more critical success factors are missing:

- numerous requests for changes to the project scope, timescale, budget or quality objectives
- push-back from the users or those affected by the project
- missing of milestones, overspending or poor quality of deliverables
- arguments between the project manager and key stakeholders
- reducing numbers or poor behaviour at team meetings.

Organisational change management

It may not be immediately obvious why the topic of organisational (business) change management has been included in a chapter on project success. Project success relies on creating outputs, then transforming those outputs into outcomes that allow benefits to be realised. This invariably requires changing ways of working within the business so they can create the desired outcomes from the project outputs. For example, there is no point in a project delivering a new IT system that meets all requirements, on time and to budget, if the people who need to use the system do not want to and find a workaround.

In some organisations projects are still focused on delivering outputs only, and the responsibilities for the changes necessary for the outputs to deliver beneficial outcomes are outside the project within the business. This was the traditional way of doing things 15 years ago when we wrote the first edition of this book. It is increasingly the case, however, that the scope of a project includes all the work necessary to create beneficial outcomes. As a result, the 'softer' skills of organisational change management are becoming increasingly integrated with the more traditional 'technical' or 'hard' aspects of project management. Where this is the case, business change experts are included in the project team in the same way as technical designers are part of the team.

More information on organisational change management is included in Chapter 30.

12

Business case

The business case sets out why the project should be undertaken, and is the main deliverable of the Concept (initiation) phase of the project life cycle. It contains all the information necessary to enable an assessment of a project proposal by an organisation's decision makers so they can make a reasoned decision on whether to invest in the project. The business case should therefore be written after a wide-ranging assessment of the costs, benefits and risks of the proposed project. It must provide as much information as necessary to enable the decision-making process.

Ownership of a business case

The sponsor owns the business case and it is their responsibility to ensure that it is developed and produced. They may delegate this task to the project manager

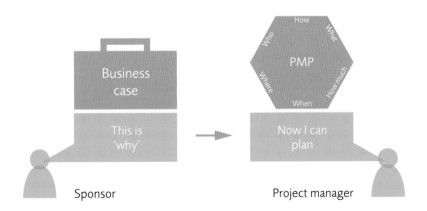

Figure 12.1 Purpose of the business case

or other members of the project team to write the document on their behalf. The business case must be formally approved by the sponsor, but may also have other signatories from the steering group (project board) and/or from other parts of the organisation, such as an enterprise programme management office or finance department. Once the business case is approved, the project can proceed into the more detailed planning or Definition phase and the preparation of the project management plan (PMP) described in the next section.

The purpose and content of the business case

The business case summarises the rationale of 'why' the project should be considered and the forecasted benefits that will come from its successful completion. Because the business case justifies the investment in the project on behalf of the organisation, it will often contain financial figures relating to:

- costs of implementing the project
- ongoing costs relating to the operation of the deliverables (if appropriate)
- benefits expected after the successful delivery of the project (for example increased income or reduced costs)
- the uncertainty associated with the estimates for costs and benefits
- some form of investment appraisal.

A business case will also contain a statement of the project's cost, time and quality objectives, as well as other relevant success criteria. Assumptions being made by project stakeholders should be included along with known constraints and issues, and the first attempt at identifying threats and opportunities (risks). In many cases there are a number of different ways that an organisation could achieve the same or similar objectives. Where alternative solutions have been considered, they are also referred to in the business case so the organisation has a historical record of why a particular approach was chosen.

A business case is most often presented as a document using a series of standard headings and supported by financial analysis. Alternatively, for a smaller project, a business case might be just a short statement with very little formal structure.

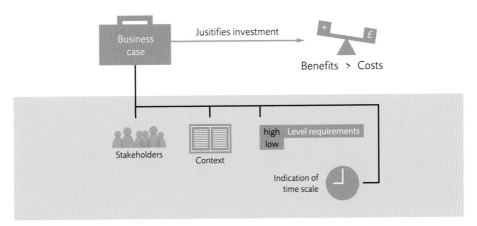

Figure 12.2 Contents of the business case

For example, in order to meet government legislation, a company needs to review and revise all of its policies relating to the hiring and firing of staff. The work must be completed by 31 March 2020. It must be in accordance with the relevant quality standards and current employee legislation. Failure to meet the required completion date will leave the company open to a substantial fine and damage to its reputation. In such a situation there is no financial justification performed or options analysed. The project is a 'must-do', or compliance project, for the organisation.

The business case should always be referred to throughout the project, especially during the change control process. The project team must be able to validate and confirm that the business case can still be met at all times.

Investment appraisal

A project is an investment, which invariably means spending money in order to gain more money (income or savings) in return. In simple terms, the amount spent should be less than the improvement received. However, it is never that simple and there are many factors that need to be taken into account when appraising the project, including the availability of money to spend and how long it takes to receive the income and also how long for.

The simplest method of investment appraisal is **payback**. This method assumes that the income from the project will exceed the up-front expenditure and looks at how soon after completion of the project (all outputs delivered) the money spent will be returned. Generally, the faster this happens the more attractive the project.

The time taken to deliver projects can vary enormously, from weeks to many years. In addition, the time taken to realise the benefit from a project can again vary enormously. If the project is to take place over multiple years, the time value of money needs to be considered. Basically, what this is saying is that a pound today is likely to be worth less in the future or if a loaf of bread costs £1 today, in the future it is likely to cost more than £1 (assuming inflation in the economy). There are a number of appraisal techniques that take into account the time value of money, such as **net present value (NPV)** and **internal rate of return (IRR)**. The mathematics behind these techniques are not important for anyone starting out in project management, but an understanding that a project must make economic sense over time is important.

In most projects of any size or complexity, the business case will contain an investment appraisal of the project, often comparing the chosen solution to other options that were discarded, perhaps because they were economically less attractive.

Funding

All projects require **funding** in some way. Sometimes the funds appear 'free' when only internal resources are used (although of course they are not really free to the organisation if someone is working on a project rather than doing something else of use). In most situations, money (capital) needs to be provided in order to carry out the project. It is the business case that provides the justification for this funding.

It is important when starting a project to have the necessary funds available or obtain a guarantee that they will be. Projects can be funded internally to the organisation or externally through things like grants, loans, joint ventures or other mechanisms such as a private finance initiative (PFI) or public private partnerships (PPP). If a project is funded internally from departmental budgets, the sponsor of the project may be the person who owns the budget. If a larger project spans multiple departments, it is the sponsor's responsibility to secure the necessary funds from budget holders. When a project is funded externally it is again the sponsor's role to ensure that all funds are either available or guaranteed. It would be wrong, if not illegal, to commence any project without appropriate funding in place.

Project Children's Hospice (PCH)

The business case for the project at its simplest level is based upon a judgement that the benefits to the charity, combined with the opportunity for staff to be socially involved and the company to be seen to be as supportive, outweigh the costs to the organisation in terms of direct and indirect costs. No investment appraisal will be carried out, as this is deemed unnecessary due to the nature of the project. The project will be funded from the revenue of your company. No additional or external funding will be required.

The definition (planning) phase

Introduction

In this phase of the project life cycle, the project manager takes forward what has been learned and agreed about the project in the business case to create detailed plans. There are a number of elements of an overall project plan and each element is covered in this section.

The objective of the Definition phase is to set up the project for success during delivery. To do this, the project plans created during this phase need to be in enough detail for the project to be formally agreed as complete and correct (project managers talk about plans being 'baselined'). This will also enable agreements and contracts that inspire confidence across the whole project team, including with suppliers.

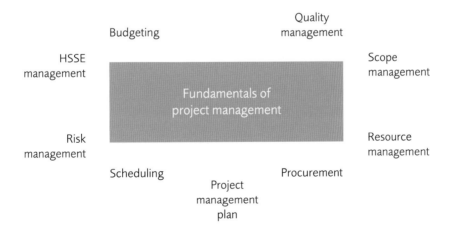

Figure 13.1 Definition (planning) phase – overview

13

Scope management

The scope of the project is central, as can be seen by its position in the middle of the project manager's 'trilemma' (see Figure 1.5). This makes the task of defining and managing project scope extremely important as the basis for the other planning processes that follow.

A project's scope is the sum of the work content of a project – in other words, all the things that need to be done in order to deliver the outputs and outcomes detailed in the business case. This means that the definition of project scope must build from the statement of requirements and reflect the project success criteria.

It is important that a project manager has a clear understanding of the scope of the project and that this understanding is communicated to the team and all stakeholders. Any subsequent changes to scope can then be managed and uncontrolled **scope creep** can be avoided. When thinking about the scope for a project, it is wise to consider not only the things that need to be done, but also the things that will not be done. This helps to remove any possible ambiguity about the project deliverables. For example, the scope of the project might be to design, build and construct a new extension for a client's house including all electrical and plumbing work, but that might exclude obtaining planning permission, or painting and decorating. By stating that the project will not seek planning permission, the client will avoid making a potentially catastrophic assumption about the work to be undertaken on their behalf.

A project's scope is directly linked to specified time, cost and quality objectives. As already mentioned, the area inside the project management triangle (see Figure 1.5) also represents the project scope. The greater the scope, the longer a project will take and the more it will cost.

When it comes to quality (or performance) the link is potentially confusing but very important. Any reduction in scope may affect the ultimate quality of the project and mean that success criteria may not be achieved. This should not happen if the project manager and sponsor (client) have a good understanding of scope, and of the relative priorities of time, cost and quality.

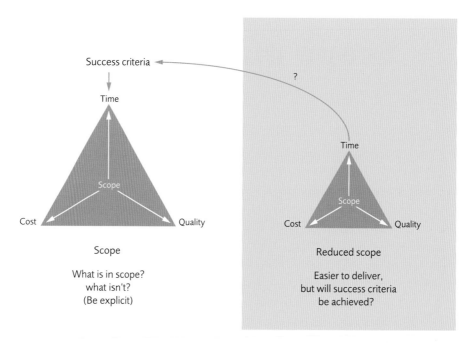

Figure 13.2 Project scope and objectives

Project Children's Hospice (PCH)

The scope of the project is to do all the things necessary to achieve the project's objectives. One key aspect of the scope to be defined is the number of different games you will have that will balance the need for maximum involvement of staff within the budget. You and your team believe that the right number of games to host is three if the objectives and success criteria as defined above are to be met.

If any of the project's objectives were changed this would have a direct influence on the project's scope. It is extremely unlikely that the date will be changed because many groups are involved, but any change in the date would cause havoc with the project's objectives. If the sponsor decided to reduce the amount of free company time available to, say, 500 hours, this would certainly mean that having three games with diverse appeal would no longer be viable. This would, in turn, mean that raising £10,000 is less likely.

Scope management involves identifying and defining all the elements of the project scope, and for keeping the scope current at all times with a clear definition of what is in scope and what is out. Scope creep is a major problem on some projects and the project manager protects the scope, or changes it only after proper review, using a change control process as described in Chapter 24.

Decomposing scope into manageable chunks

Project managers use a range of different breakdown structures to literally 'break-down' or decompose the project into more detailed parts. They provide an essential structure for project planning, monitoring and control. There are four primary breakdown structures that are commonly used during core project planning. These are: product breakdown structure (PBS), work breakdown structure (WBS), cost breakdown structure (CBS) and organisation breakdown structure (OBS). For some smaller/simpler projects, the use of one of these breakdown structures would be sufficient. For larger/more complex projects, the project manager is likely to use multiple breakdown structures in order to define scope sufficiently.

The **product breakdown structure (PBS)** is a hierarchy of products (another term for deliverables or project outputs) that are required to be produced to complete the project. A PBS uses nouns (names of deliverables at various levels). It is usual convention for the whole project to be referred to as Level 0 and then each subsequent breakdown of the project to be referred to as Level 1, Level 2, Level 3 etc. The lowest level of a PBS is a distinct project output, such as desks or telephones.

The **work breakdown structure (WBS)** is slightly different in that it is a hierarchy that leads to the work that needs to be done to complete the project. A WBS uses verbs and nouns (things that need to be done at various levels). The lowest level of a WBS is either called a **work package** or alternatively an **activity**, such as install desks or install telephones.

One commonly used approach to define project scope is to start with a PBS to identify the main products, then at a certain level of definition further break down those products into packages of work that can be assigned to project team members to perform. This combined technique can be the most useful way of ensuring that all the work to be done is captured.

Whatever technique is used (PBS, WBS or combined PBS/WBS), the objective is to define the scope of the project completely and in sufficient detail so that team members can do the work. It is particularly important when considering if *all* the work has been defined to include all the generic project management work and products (such as the project management plan), as well as all the specific technical work and specialist products for the project in question. When we talk about project outputs, we mean the delivery of all the scope to meet the specified requirements and to the right standards of quality and regulatory compliance.

Irrespective of the technique used, each 'box' in the breakdown structure should be uniquely identified with a code.

Project Children's Hospice (PCH)

The breakdown structure in Figure 13.3 is a combined PBS and WBS for the project. The boxes on the white background are the project's products or deliverables and the boxes on the shaded background are the project's activities or work packages.

The **cost breakdown structure (CBS)** also represents the work of the project but this time organised as a hierarchical breakdown of cost elements. This is of particular use when organising budgets and allocating expenditure for work in a way that can be dealt with and reported in a sensible manner by the management accountants.

The **organisational breakdown structure (OBS)** also represents the work of the project but this time organised as a hierarchical breakdown of the management groups and resources involved in the project. An OBS often resembles an organisation chart and shows the project organisation in enough detail for work to be allocated to groups, units or individuals.

Both the CBS and OBS increase in complexity depending on the number of levels that are defined in the original PBS, WBS or combined PBS/WBS.

Using a Responsibility Assignment Matrix (RAM)

All projects involve more than one person, or the work would simply be a task. Most projects involve tens of different people, many of who are from different departments, functions or even organisations, such as suppliers or contractors or external regulatory bodies. In the world of project management, the sponsor is accountable for delivering the business benefits and the project manager is accountable for delivering the project as agreed in the project management plan according to its time, cost and quality objectives. Being accountable, however,

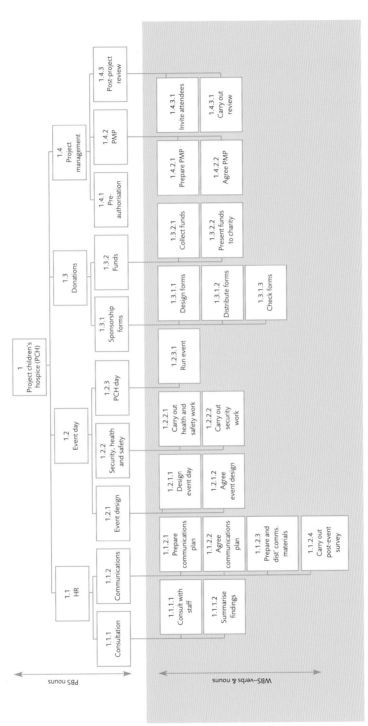

Figure 13.3 Product breakdown structure/work breakdown structure (PBS/WBS) for PCH

doesn't mean that either the sponsor or the project manager has sole responsibility for doing the work.

A **responsibility assignment matrix or RAM** is used to define who in the organisation of the project is responsible for each of the project's deliverables. It is a grid along two dimensions, which combines the project's work breakdown structure (or product breakdown structure) along one axis, with its organisation breakdown structure along the other axis. In each cell of the grid (see Figure 13.4) a coding structure is used to determine the relative involvement of each party in each product or piece of work.

A typical coding system might be:

- R – responsible
- A – accountable (or approval)
- C – consult
- I – inform.

	Sponsor	Project manager	Health and safety officer	Security adviser	Games managers	Finance manager	Quality manager
Consultation	R	A/R	I	I	C	I	C
Communication	C	A/R	C	C	C	I	C
Event design	C	A	C	C	R	I	C
Health and safety	I	A	R	C	C	I	C
Security	I	A	C	R	C	I	C
PCH day	A	R	C	C	R	I	I
Sponsorship forms	C	A/R	I	I	C	C	C
Funds	A	C	I	I	I	R	I
PMP	C	A/R	C	C	C	C	C
Post-project review	C	A/R	C	C	C	C	C

OBS (horizontal axis). PBS or WBS (vertical axis).

Figure 13.4 Responsibility assignment matrix for PCH

An example using the above coding might be the project's end-of-project report. The project manager is *accountable* for this. They may choose to delegate this *responsibility* to the project management office, who in turn will *consult* with the sponsor and other stakeholders when preparing it. All other team members will be *informed* of the outcome. Some organisations use other coding structures that may relate to a particular function; for example, in engineering, D might be used for design, C for checking and I for inspection.

The purpose of a responsibility assignment matrix is to ensure that all members of the team are aware of their responsibilities and how they fit into the broader picture of the project. It will also avoid the risk that no one takes total responsibility for certain products or work, or that key consultations or checks are missed.

Managing scope throughout the project

As outlined above, defining scope in detail is the first step of the Definition (planning) phase of the project life cycle. We will explore how this definition of scope is taken forward to create complete project management plans that will enable the project's time, cost and quality objectives to be met.

This is not the last time the project manager needs to think about scope. All changes to scope need to be agreed and documented and the plans that are built on this also amended. This process is carried out under change control once the project plans have been formally accepted and baselined at the end of the Definition phase. This is vital because when the project reaches the end of Delivery and is preparing to Handover the project outputs to the sponsor/client, a key check will be whether all the scope has been delivered, to the right quality (and in what time, for what cost).

14

Quality management

Quality forms one of the dimensions of the time, cost and quality triangle, the project manager's 'trilemma', and as such needs to be rigorously and proactively managed. There is no point in delivering something on time and to budget that nobody wants, likes or can use.

What is quality and what is quality management?

The most common way of defining the quality of a deliverable or product is to say that it must be 'fit for purpose'. This means that it meets the stated requirements – no more, no less. Quality is not about 'doing the best you can' or 'excellence' in any way. It is about defining the standards that need to be achieved and then doing it – reliably and consistently. In projects, therefore, quality management is the discipline applied to all work that is done to make sure that the deliverables from projects are fit for purpose.

As discussed in Chapter 13, deliverables or outputs from projects will include:

- specialist, or 'technical' products or services, such as a mobile telephone made to a new design or a management report from the Definition phase of the project
- management products, such as records that provide evidence of how the project management processes were managed, for example the project's business case, the project management plan or the **risk log** etc.

It is a fact that the standard that is achieved for every deliverable will be of concern to at least one stakeholder. Achieving stakeholder requirements is the principle that drives the quality management process. When requirements are understood, acceptance criteria can be developed for each deliverable or product. With acceptance criteria in place, plans can be made to ensure that results are achieved and can be demonstrated.

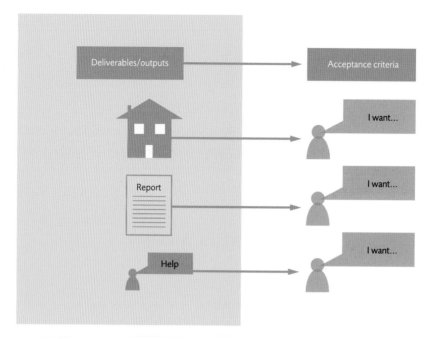

Figure 14.1 Fit for purpose

You will notice that project quality management is not about compliance with quality management standards such as ISO 9001:2015. Such a standard is a good way for an organisation to control processes and the project management process for your organisation may be controlled using such a system. Compliance with ISO 9001: 2015 must not be confused with project quality management that is about ensuring that specific deliverables meet specific objectives for change.

Project Children's Hospice (PCH)

There are many deliverables from the project that need to be fit for purpose. Three examples are:

1 fundraising games to take place on the day in your offices, although note that the number of games have not yet been finalised
2 correctly completed sponsorship forms
3 an agreed plan for the day.

Acceptance criteria for these three deliverables have been agreed as follows:

1 The organisation and delivery of each game must actively involve 10 people to organise and run it, and attract a minimum of 20 other staff to attend. Each game must take place safely and without upsetting anyone, and cater for staff with physical disabilities.
2 All sponsorship forms should contain the sponsoring person's name, department or address and telephone number, and a clear statement of the amount donated. All writing should be in ink and must be legible.
3 An agreed plan for the day, including a schedule of games, must be prepared and agreed by the sponsor and project team within six weeks.

As part of your planning for the project you need to involve the company's health and safety officer when designing the event and the individual games. You will ask him to make sure that each event can be carried out safely and you are prepared to accept his recommendations for any changes. You have also arranged to meet with him on a weekly basis to review all aspects of the project.

To check that the sponsorship forms are being filled in correctly you have asked each of your team to carry out random reviews of forms being used within their departments. If they find any forms that are poorly completed they will encourage the form owner to correct the deficiency.

The four elements of quality management

Managing quality has four main elements – quality planning, quality assurance, quality control and continual improvement.

Quality planning is the process for determining which quality standards are applicable to the project and how to apply them. Quality standards may relate to the industry sector, for example compliance with QS 9000 in the automotive sector. They may also apply to the organisation, i.e. compulsory company standards or quality policy, or to a client organisation, i.e. to supply to the client evidence of control to ISO 9001 standards. Once the standards are understood, plans to achieve them must be made and documented in a quality plan. The quality plan forms a key part of the overall project management plan (PMP).

Some organisations treat specific health, safety, security and environmental (HSSE) standards as inputs to the quality planning process; this is good practice. We cover HSSE more fully in Chapter 15.

Quality assurance is needed to evaluate the overall project performance on a periodic basis to provide confidence that the process is effective and that objectives will be met. The principal way of achieving this is through periodic quality audits, using people independent of the project delivery team to check that processes and ways of working meet stated requirements. Specific work results are not checked as part of quality assurance, the purpose is to review whether the underlying processes and ways of working are leading towards product deliverables of the right quality. The project manager must then consider and action the recommendations made by the auditor. This role is often performed by a part of the project organisation called 'project assurance'. In some organisations this is outsourced to an independent party to provide confidence to the steering group that the project is being well managed.

The strategy for quality assurance is typically described in the quality plan section of the PMP for the project, e.g. to outline who will conduct audits, to what scope, when and where.

Quality control verifies that the specific project deliverables comply to the quality standards outlined in the quality plan and the acceptance criteria for the deliverables. Quality control may be achieved by physically inspecting or checking particular items, for instance, **peer review** of design calculations or a piece of marketing literature, or testing computer code or the integrity of a weld. Alternatively, it can be achieved through surveying a group of people, e.g. to find out if employees are satisfied following a reorganisation, a questionnaire or focus groups could be used.

A key part of quality management associated with quality control is to find out the causes of any errors or problems and to address these so they don't happen again. This approach leads to the final step in a quality management process – continual (or continuous) improvement.

Continual improvement, often referred to as 'Kaizen' due to the Japanese management techniques from which the practice originated, is more than a technique. It is the culture and planned systematic approach to improvement that needs to be created to ensure that lessons are learned and that the root causes of problems are identified and managed so that a mistake is never made twice.

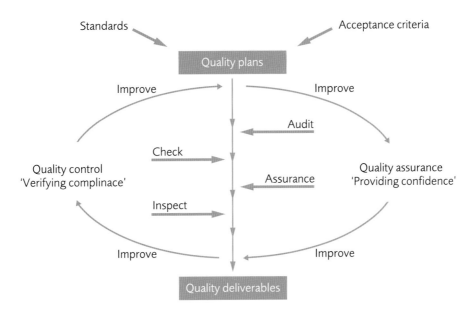

Figure 14.2 Elements of quality management

Continual improvement can apply within one project, particularly a project with a large scope that is expected to have a duration of many years. Often, however, continual improvement relating to projects applies at programme or portfolio level, where the organisation needs to put in place practices to ensure that learning from one project is applied in other projects.

15

Health, safety, security and environmental (HSSE) management

Many organisations will take account of specific requirements to manage the health and safety of people, the security of physical locations and/or of data, and the impact of the project on the physical environment as part of quality planning. When this happens, the quality plans in the overall project management plan will include all the work to ensure that relevant regulations, standards and stakeholder expectations are met. Other organisations, particularly those in sectors where project work has the potential for significant impact on HSSE matters, will create separate plans to make it clear to the project team what they should do to meet required standards.

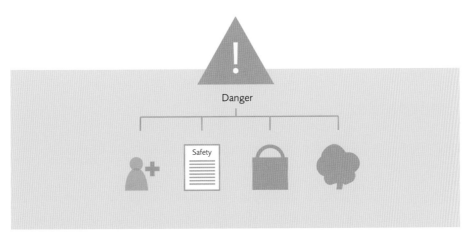

Figure 15.1 Health, safety, security and environmental (HSSE) in practice

Health and safety

Every country has its own specific legislation that outlines the requirements to protect people from harm at work, and to outline the responsibilities of the employee as well as the employer. As a minimum, relevant legislation will include the requirement for employers to provide relevant personal protective equipment, and for employees to wear it in specified areas. Many organisations have invested heavily in approaches to **health and safety management** with a focus on 'zero harm' and here the requirements of the project team are likely to go way beyond those specified in law, e.g. the requirement to intervene if you see another person acting in an unsafe manner. It is the responsibility of the project manager to understand the law and the requirements of the performing organisation, plus any explicit requirements or expectations of external stakeholders. Health and safety plans in the overall PMP must apply to the whole supply chain so that there are consistent standards for how people are treated on the project.

Security

Security can apply to physical facilities related to the project, e.g. the office where the team is working or the location where any physical facilities will be built, and applies to the security of project information and data. In the same way as for health and safety, the project manager must understand relevant legislation, as well as expectations of stakeholders, and then make plans to comply.

Environment

In HSSE, the term environment tends to be used to describe the physical world, with environmental management objectives relating to minimising the negative effects of the project on air quality, water courses, noise levels etc. To do this, legislation must be understood, plus any other requirements of the performing organisation to drive down impact on the environment beyond statutory levels. This is not to be confused with the use of the term environment to refer to the project's context, i.e. the people, organisations or practices that might have an effect on the project or vice versa.

On large projects, or within project organisations in companies that have inherent HSSE risks, e.g. construction, energy and natural resources, chemicals manufacture etc., the project is likely to have a specific HSSE/compliance expert/ team of experts allocated from a specialist department. Where this is not the case, the project manager retains responsibility for ensuring that the project has adequate plans to safeguard the health, safety and security of people, the security of data and the integrity of the physical environment in which we all live and operate.

Project Children's Hospice (PCH)

Your company is committed to creating a safe place to work for all employees and doing everything possible to protect the environment. The games you arrange as part of the overall event must be organised in a way that no one can get hurt and that security of the company's property and data is safe-guarded. You also must not do things that would cause pollution of any kind, including excessive noise. You are going to allocate the responsibility for HSSE compliance to one of your team members.

16

Risk management

The simplest definition of a **project risk** is an uncertainty that matters; it is about trying to anticipate the future and protect the project as far as possible from things that might happen. Formal risk management is considered by many experts in project management as the most beneficial technique on the basis that plans are 'educated guesses' and therefore all there is to manage is what might happen that would cause actual performance to vary from the plan. If the project team just takes a chance that nothing bad will happen, it is likely that the project will require a degree of crisis management. Managing risk is intended to proactively avoid crises and to seize opportunities to do things even better.

There is never a correct place to put risk management in the project life cycle. The project sponsor and project manager need to think about risk early in the life cycle, as a key input to the business case. They also need to think about risk 'here', i.e. when scope and associated quality and HSSE requirements have been understood, and before time, resource and cost planning. The most important message, though, is that the project manager needs to be engaging others to identify, own and manage risk throughout the project life cycle.

Risks to project objectives

A risk is an uncertain situation or event that *may* occur, which, if it does, *will* impact on one or more of the project's objectives, e.g. time, cost, quality or another of the project's success criteria. A key responsibility of the project manager is to understand individual risks (situations or events that may occur) and manage them to optimise the effect on the project and its stakeholders. Current thinking in project management is that risks can be both threats, i.e. things that would jeopardise the ability to meet objectives if they occurred, or opportunities, i.e. things that would enhance the ability to meet objectives if they occurred. The project manager also needs to think about overall project risk (as opposed to individual risky events). This will be explored further later in the chapter.

There is often confusion between project risks and project issues. Both risks and issues affect project objectives but a risk is something that might happen and an issue is something that is happening, i.e. there is no uncertainty. Issue management is covered in Chapter 23.

Any project that is undertaken will contain risks because no one can reliably know what might happen in the future. Just as no one knows what numbers will win the Lotto next week, no one knows exactly how a project will turn out. The purpose of risk management is to make projects less of a lottery so that achievement of specific objectives for change is more certain.

Typical risks on projects often relate to uncertain resource availability or uncertainties about the environment in which the project will take place. Examples of risks in these areas might be as follows:

- There may not be enough IT testing resource available to test the final system.
- Current employees may not have the skills required to work with the new technology.
- Our ideal project team may be available and things will be done quicker than planned.
- Planning permission may take longer to obtain than scheduled.
- A change in government may mean a change in policy, making the project invalid.
- We may have an unseasonal dry spell that would mean that the outdoor painting could be completed faster.

To manage risk, the project manager needs to carry out a structured process that enables individual risks and overall project risk to be identified, understood and

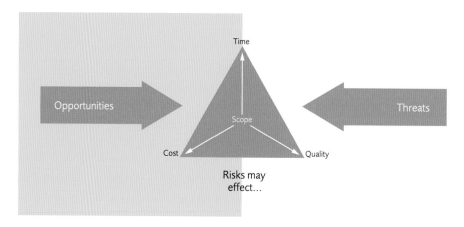

Figure 16.1 Risks can be opportunities or threats

managed proactively, optimising project success by minimising threats and maximising opportunities.

Risks don't just exist for large or complex projects. All projects are susceptible to uncertainty and so risk management should be carried out regardless of project size. It is clear, though, that risk management isn't 'free' in a real sense. The effort put into managing the risk process costs the project money, and taking action to respond to identified risks will also cost money. The process is usually deemed to be beneficial, however.

The benefits of risk management that outweigh costs include the following:

- Issues and problems cost more to solve than the costs of preventing them occurring.
- Plans are more accurate because estimates have taken account of risks.
- Stakeholders are more confident that plans are realistic and can be delivered.

Project Children's Hospice (PCH)

There are a number of obvious risks associated with the project. Five of these are:

- You may be unable to secure enough volunteers to organise and run the actual games on the day.
- An important company project may require that a key resource cannot meet their project obligations.
- There may be more interest in the project than anticipated, resulting in an 'oversubscription' of the games planned.
- Someone may get hurt in one of the games.
- Someone may take offence at one of the games.

As project manager, you need to deal with these risks; they may well happen and, if they do, they will impact the project. The 'costs' of trying to manage the risks are very likely to be significantly less than the 'costs' of dealing with one or more issues if the risks are ignored, but you need to keep this in mind and make sure you do not spend too much time and money trying to make the project 'risk free'.

You have identified a number of risks for the project but nothing further has been done. Focusing on the risk that 'you may be unable to secure enough volunteers to organise and run the actual games on the day', you should probably consider this to be an important risk as it could seriously affect the amount you can raise and the whole spectacle of the day. As it is important you may want to reduce the risk of it occurring by making sure that potential volunteers get plenty of notice. You may also try to think of incentives that might attract them to take part, such as personally meeting the celebrity you have invited and hope will attend.

You need to find a **risk owner** for the risk. You decide you will take this role on this occasion but there are other risks that have been identified where you need someone else to be the risk owner.

The important thing to remember when it comes to risk management is that unless you actually do something, like giving plenty of notice or offering other incentives, you have not changed the risk at all, i.e. you haven't carried out risk management.

One of the risks you identified, 'there may be more interest in the project than anticipated', should ideally be owned by your boss as the sponsor. This risk is an opportunity in that the more people who are interested will increase the money you raise. The risk owner (sponsor) needs to decide how to make this happen. Ignoring it will change nothing whereas making some more company time available would enhance the chance significantly.

A typical project risk management process

It is one thing to identify risks, but just identifying them does not do anything for the success of the project. Unlike a lottery, where the outcome is truly uncertain, in most cases there are things that can be done to:

- affect whether a risk occurs or not
- influence how much of an impact it might have on a project if it occurs.

In order to do this, it is beneficial to carry out risk management in a consistent manner.

A typical **risk management process** would follow the steps listed below:

- **Initiate** the risk management process. Focus on the objectives that are 'at risk' and decide how the project will work to ensure that risk management identifies the priority risks and manages them to improve the chances of successful project delivery.
- **Identify** risks (both threats and opportunities), describing them in such a way that stakeholders can understand what is uncertain and how it would affect objectives.
- **Assess** the risks to see whether they are important or worth worrying about. This is usually done by thinking about the likelihood (probability) of the risk occurring and the size of impact if it did, and coming up with a risk score, which is a combination of the two.
- For those risks that are considered to be important, think of what could be done to **respond** to the risk in order to change the chance that it will occur and the impact it would have on project objectives. Some **risk responses** are focused on changing the likelihood of the risk occurring – when these apply to a threat they are often called risk mitigations (mitigate meaning 'to soften'). Other

Figure 16.2 A project risk management process

responses might be to share the risk in the supply chain or with an insurer so that if the risk occurs not all the impact is borne by the organisation investing in the project. For low-priority risks, the project manager will probably decide to take the chance and make no response other than to monitor the situation.

■ Finally, make sure that the responses that were agreed above actually take place.

The risk management process doesn't only happen once on a project. It should be carried out during the project Definition phase and then repeated throughout the life of the project.

One key part of a project risk management process is the assignment of people to be risk owners for each risk that is identified. The project manager always retains responsibility for the overall process, but they are not the person who is best placed to deal with every risk, nor to 'watch' the situation as the project progresses. Organisations who manage risks well understand the need for committed risk owners to be in place.

The use of a risk log

All identified risks should be recorded in a risk log (some people call it a risk register – there is no difference). A risk log is a formal record of all identified risks and it contains information such as:

■ a description of the risk
■ its chance of occurrence (likelihood or probability)
■ its likely impact
■ who the risk owner is
■ what response (action) the risk owner intends to take.

The risk log also records when the risk has either occurred (and become an issue) or is no longer a risk for the project. It should be maintained through all phases of the project life cycle.

As any action that is taken on the project can affect the ability to achieve time, cost and quality objectives and the wider success criteria, it is critical that risk owners work in partnership with the project manager. This is to ensure that decisions taken are in the best interest of the project as a whole. In particular, the risk log should highlight any constraints on risk owners: for example, the

Id	Description	Probability	Impact	Owner	Response/action	Status
1	There are a lot of fundraising events taking place at the moment. Staff and friends may be unwilling to contribute donations to this event. This will lead to less money being donated to the PCH charity.	L	H	Sponsor	Stress the importance of the PCH charity and also that.. 'Every little bit counts'	Current
2	The PCH charity event will be covered by a local newspaper. It may be seen as supporting worthy cause. This will lead to further interest in the charity and increased funds being donated.	M	H	Project manager	Maximise exposure in the press. Get the reporter to include lots of photography	Current
3	The event communications materials will need to developed by the in-house comms dept and they are always very busy. They might hold up the comms process. This will lead to a delay in running the event.	M	M	Project manager	Warn the comunications department that this will be required and stress its importance. Update them as to exactly when their input is needed.	Closed

Figure 16.3 A simple risk log for PCH

maximum costs they can expend dealing with a particular risk or the time by which they must achieve the desired response.

Analysis of overall project risk

The basic and foundational part of project risk management is the identification, prioritisation and management of discrete uncertain events or situations that would matter to project objectives if they occurred. Many organisations also want to consider the combined effect of all these risks with estimating uncertainty to analyse overall project risk. Techniques for doing this enable the project manager to be able to predict confidence levels in different project outcomes, for example, the chance of reaching a particular **milestone**, or the chance of delivering all the scope, to the right quality, on budget.

Analysing overall project risk requires specific technical risk management skills. Most project managers would draw on specialists to help them with the statistical analysis. The project manager, however, is the person best placed to engage stakeholders and to help them to describe what they perceive to be risky and why. All risk analysis is only as good as the input data, and this comes from people, not software packages.

17

Estimating

To plan anything, we need to make estimates about things that will happen in the future. In projects we are estimating how many people will be needed to carry out a task (effort) or how long the task might take (duration), as well as how much money we might spend on people, or other things we buy or consume in completing the scope of work.

Our project plans, based on estimates, are in fact 'educated guesses'. They can never be accurate, i.e. the project finishes all the work, to the right quality, on exactly the day you said and for exactly the cost you said, unless perhaps you have been very lucky. It is best not to use the words accurate and estimate in the same breath. However, we do want to make our estimate as accurate (reliable) as possible so that stakeholders have confidence in our plans. It follows that anything that can be done to improve estimates and make guesses as 'educated as practically possible' is worth the effort.

You may be thinking that there is a close link between risk management and estimating, and you would be correct. We are unable to make accurate estimates because there are too many things that we do not know. Some of these things are just plain estimating uncertainty, for example, we just don't know how productive our team of workers will actually be. In addition, there are many 'what-ifs' or 'if this, then thats' – these make it difficult for us to predict what will happen with any certainty.

But we have no option – we need to make estimates – so there are some techniques that we can use to do the best job possible.

The estimating funnel

We said that it is not advisable to talk about the accuracy of estimates but we do need a language to explain to stakeholders how confident they should be in our estimates. That language is to talk about ranges (the range of expected outcomes).

Estimating is most difficult at the start of the project when there is lots of uncertainty about what is to be done, when, by whom etc. An estimate prepared at the beginning of the project is likely to have a wide range when compared to an estimate prepared during the last phases of a project when its detail is more clearly understood. The most important thing to do early in the life cycle is to document the underpinning assumptions associated with estimates. Keeping a record of assumptions helps build a common understanding across the team. It is also important to monitor these assumptions as things change – to ensure that plans are not built on false assumptions.

It is quite normal to update estimates throughout the life cycle of the project. Perhaps the most important estimate is that which accompanies the project management plan (PMP). This is the estimate upon which the project budget will be authorised. Many organisations look for an estimate that has a range of only plus or minus 10 per cent at this point. Others use techniques to express the confidence level in a point estimate, for example a 50 per cent confidence of achieving a certain date. To do this, quite sophisticated risk analysis is needed, as explained in Chapter 16.

The idea that estimates improve as the project progresses through the life cycle is often called the **estimating funnel**.

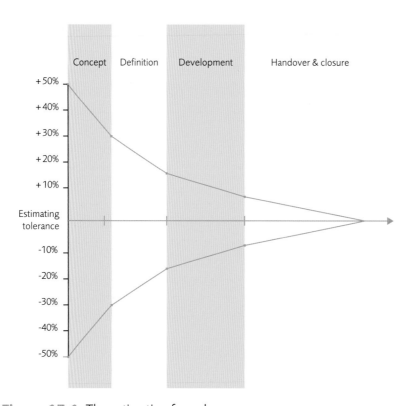

Figure 17.1 The estimating funnel

Estimating methods

There are four main estimating methods that can be used: **bottom-up estimating**, **comparative estimating**, **parametric estimating** and **three-point estimating**.

The only technique that can be used if the organisation has no prior experience of doing a project like the one being estimated is to use bottom-up estimating. This requires the preparation of a work breakdown structure (WBS), or a combined product/work breakdown structure (PBS/WBS) for the project down to a level of detail that allows a cost to be estimated by the 'owner' of each work package or activity. The individual estimates are then summed to give the total estimate for the project.

Bottom-up estimating takes time, whereas comparative estimating is relatively quick if the organisation has some relevant past experience. A comparative estimate uses more of a 'top-down' approach. To prepare a comparative estimate, the current project is compared to others like it, while at the same time asking questions such as:

- Is it bigger or smaller than the ones we are comparing with?
- Is it more or less complex?
- Is it using the same technology or design methods?

Using this approach, the answer might be that it is twice as big as the last similar project, a little more complex and uses improved design methods. Therefore, the answer chosen might be to multiply the cost of the last project by two to create the estimate for the new project.

Another method of estimating if the organisation has data from past similar projects relies on the use of key parameters or measures and is known as parametric estimating. The parameters are fed into a model to create an estimate. Examples of parametric estimating are often found in the IT industry. Typical parameters might be the number of data entry screens or the number of reports to be prepared. If values for these parameters, as well as a few others, are fed into a model, it will then generate an estimate of how much effort is required to complete the work using the assumption that all the other elements of the work will be related to the chosen key parameters in some way. Parametric estimating requires an organisation to hold a considerable amount of historic data about the work to be done and to keep it up-to-date. As a result, some projects don't have the option of using this method – but if the data exists, it absolutely should be used.

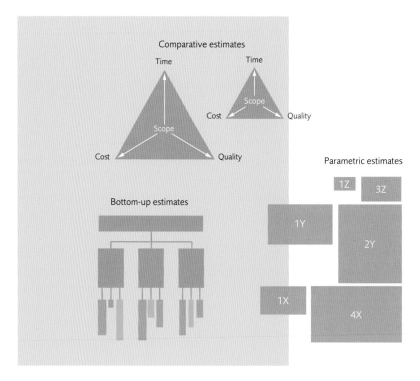

Figure 17.2 Different methods of estimating

Project Children's Hospice (PCH)

You have put together initial plans for the project but haven't completed work on the project management plan (PMP). The plans so far contain a number of estimates particularly relating to the duration of project activities and the amount of effort (primarily yours) that will be required. These original estimates will be refined as part of the preparation of the PMP.

It will not be possible to come up with a definitive estimate until after the individual games have been designed, five weeks into the project.

You have never worked on a project like this before but the PBS/WBS you have developed has allowed you to carry out bottom-up estimating. The lack of experience means that there is no data to carry out a comparative or parametric estimate. At least in the future, should the company want to do something similar, the data from this project will allow an overall comparative estimate to be used at the start and for parametric estimates to be established for key aspects of the project. Examples might be the amount\of staff time used in ratio to the number of games, or the ratio between the number of games and the amount of money raised.

Three-point estimating can be used in conjunction with any of the other three methods and in conjunction with the risk information in the risk log. The idea of a three-point estimate is that you estimate the range of possible outcomes for a specific work activity (if used in conjunction with bottom-up estimating), or the whole project (with comparative) or for key parameters (if using parametric) and then take a view on the most likely outcome from that range by considering the risks that contribute to the uncertain estimate.

A common example would be to think about your journey to work. You will know the quickest time that you could achieve. You will also be able to identify the threats that could occur that would make your journey time longer, and you'll be able to take an educated guess at the likelihood of those risks occurring. If they all occurred and you were really unlucky the maximum time it could take might be a very long time, but using your judgement you can estimate the most likely time. The resultant numbers – the minimum time (best case), the maximum time (worst case) and the most likely time – are the three-point estimate. To convert a three-point estimate into a single point for use in a schedule or budget, it is most usual to use something called the PERT formula (**program evaluation and review technique**) which provides a single 'weighted average' number.

$$\frac{\text{Best case} + (4 \times \text{most likely}) + \text{worst case}}{6}$$

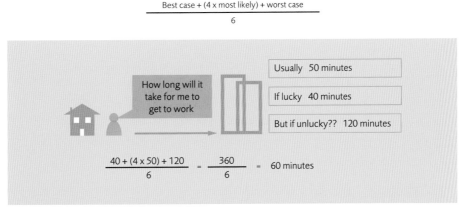

Figure 17.3 A journey to work using a three-point estimate and the PERT formula

18

Scheduling

Scheduling means planning when activities will be carried out – it is the time-based articulation of the overall project plan. Often people talk about a project plan and they mean the project schedule. In some industries/sectors the project schedule is called the programme. Be careful and ask questions to understand what people actually mean when they say project plan or programme.

Understanding scheduling involves learning the terminology associated with **critical path analysis** – the main technique associated with scheduling. Terms include network diagram, Gantt (bar) chart, critical path, total float, free float, milestones and baseline. These concepts are central to effective project planning and management and it is really important to understand them, even if on a day-to-day basis you use a computer-based tool to help you create schedules.

We are lucky to have many computer-based tools that are very intuitive to use. The downside of this is that people are often lulled into thinking that the first thing they must do to plan the project is to put together the schedule using commonly available computer software. The fact is that proper scheduling is a major help when managing a project but proper schedules can only be put together when *all the other things covered in this book up until now* are already in place.

Key concepts in scheduling

When a project manager has defined the scope of the project (the work that needs to be completed), understands quality requirements and risks, and has estimates of activity durations in place, the next step is to put together a schedule. Putting together the schedule (scheduling) enables the project manager to predict the overall project duration and when activities and events are planned to happen.

To move from a list of activities with estimates to a schedule, the project manager needs to do two more things. First, identify *logical dependencies* between activities to determine the order, or sequence, in which those activities need to be carried out. A logical dependency identifies predecessors and successors for activities. Typical dependencies used are:

■ Finish to start (activity A must finish before activity B starts).
■ Start to start (activity B can start when activity A has started).
■ Finish to finish (activity B can finish when activity A has finished).

In considering dependencies, the project manager may also use the concept of 'leads' and 'lags', for example Activity B can start two days before Activity A has finished (Finish-Start dependency with a two-day lead), or Activity B can only start three days after Activity A has finished (Finish-Start dependency with a three-day lag).

Second, the project manager needs to identify resource requirements and availability (this will be dealt with in full in Chapter 19).

The scope, estimates, logical dependencies and understanding of resource requirements, when put together, mean that the project manager can now define the sequence of work through the project. All this information is used to prepare the project network that can be done either by hand, or using a computer-based tool.

Project Children's Hospice (PCH)

Figure 18.1 is a drawing of a network for the PCH. The numbers for activities relate back to the scope definition of the PCH in Figure 13.3.

Note that it is a mistake to confuse logical dependencies and resources. We often see schedules with artificial constraints because a task has been 'fixed in

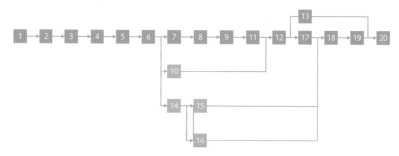

Figure 18.1 Network diagram for PCH

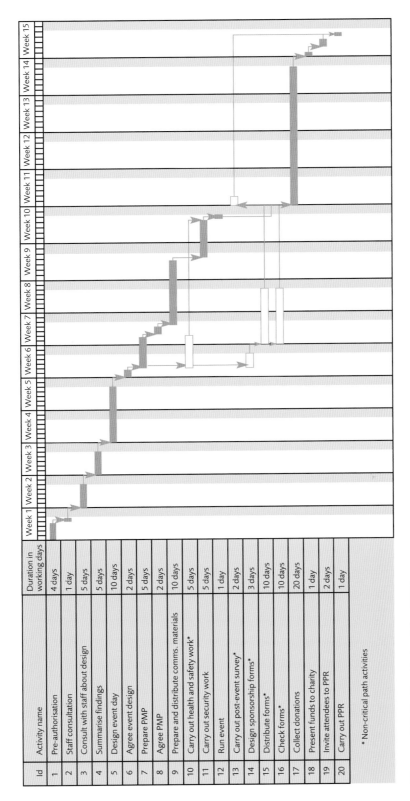

Id	Activity name	Duration in working days	Week 1	Week 2	Week 3	Week 4	Week 5	Week 6	Week 7	Week 8	Week 9	Week 10	Week 11	Week 12	Week 13	Week 14	Week 15
1	Pre-authorisation	4 days															
2	Staff consultation	1 day															
3	Consult with staff about design	5 days															
4	Summarise findings	5 days															
5	Design event day	10 days															
6	Agree event design	2 days															
7	Prepare PMP	5 days															
8	Agree PMP	2 days															
9	Prepare and distribute comms. materials	10 days															
10	Carry out health and safety work*	5 days															
11	Carry out security work	5 days															
12	Run event	1 day															
13	Carry out post-event survey*	2 days															
14	Design sponsorship forms*	3 days															
15	Distribute forms*	10 days															
16	Check forms*	10 days															
17	Collect donations	20 days															
18	Present funds to charity	1 day															
19	Invite attendees to PPR	2 days															
20	Carry out PPR	1 day															

* Non-critical path activities

Figure 18.2 Gantt chart for PCH

time' because of the availability of a resource. This may be necessary, but should be the last step in finalising the schedule and *after* resource optimisation has been done (see Chapter 19). A good schedule contains no artificial constraints.

The network diagram enables the project manager to identify the **critical path** or paths for the project.

Critical path is a term that is synonymous with project management. All projects have a critical path; some have more than one. A critical path will determine the shortest time in which a project can be completed. Another way of expressing this is to say that the critical path also represents the longest path of activity through the project. Both of these statements describe the significance of a critical path.

The purpose of a project manager understanding a project's critical path(s) is to be able to focus effort in managing the activities that lie on it with the knowledge that if all of them complete on time, and if there is no slippage on other activities that exceeds the **total float**, the whole project will finish on time.

The most common usual way of showing a project's schedule is to use a **Gantt (bar) chart** as it is relatively simple to read and understand. A Gantt chart can be as simple as a list of activities drawn against a horizontal timescale, with each activity represented by a bar that also shows the period over which it is to be carried out.

Until the mid-1970s, project scheduling was something that was done by a person by hand, using mental arithmetic. Changing the information once drawn was time-consuming. There are now various software tools that use a graphical user interface (GUI) to do the drawing and the maths and will plot the schedule information in many formats. Computer software is not needed to prepare schedules but it can be very useful.

The information contained within a project network diagram or a Gantt chart for a project is the same, it is just a different means of displaying the same information.

Clearly not all activities are on the critical path for a project. The ones that are not on the critical path have what is officially described as **float** (in the UK) or slack (in the USA). There are two different kinds of float – total float as previously mentioned and **free float**. Both total and free float relate to the amount of leeway there is in relation to when an activity needs to take place in order to maintain the overall project schedule.

Total float is the time by which an activity may be delayed or extended without affecting the total project duration whereas free float is the time by which an activity may be delayed or extended without affecting the start of any succeeding activity.

A project manager who understands which activities on their project have float and which are critical will be better able to make decisions relating to whether the start of an activity can be delayed or not.

For example, consider a project that has three sequential activities, A, B and C, that all have finish to start dependencies. Activity A has five days' total float and zero free float, B has five days' total float and five days free float and C has zero total float and free float. With this information the project manager knows that if the finish of A is delayed by three days, the owner of activity B will need to be warned that the start of their work will be delayed by three days. The project manager can still rest easy, though, as the overall project completion date will remain unaffected as A has five days' total float. Assuming now that A doesn't get delayed but, for whatever reason, it would benefit the project to delay the start and finish of B by five days. Because B has five days free float, the project manager knows that the effect of this does not need to be discussed with any other activity owner. As long as the finish of B is not delayed more than five days, the start of C is unaffected. Any delay to C will affect the end date of the project.

Another example of total float and free float is shown in Figure 18.3 for the PCH. From this you should be able to see that activity 14, 'Design sponsorship forms' has a total float of ten days but has zero free float because any delay in its completion will delay the start of Activity 15, 'Distribute forms'. Activity 20 has 10 days' total float and 10 days' free float. This means that its completion can be delayed by up to 10 days before it delays the whole project.

Once the schedule has been fully developed and included in the PMP, it is said to be 'baselined'. The baseline is the version of the schedule against which the project's time objectives will be monitored and controlled. The concept of the baseline applies equally to all aspects of the PMP, not just the schedule.

Milestones

In preparing project schedules another key technique is the use of milestones. As the name suggests, milestones indicate key points in the schedule. They represent the completion of deliverables or highlight key decision points on the project. They are not activities because they have no (zero) duration.

Milestones can simplify the communication of the schedule by reporting the status of the project at a summary level. This kind of communication is essential for senior management or other parties who may not necessarily be interested in the detail of the project, but are interested in its outcome and progress.

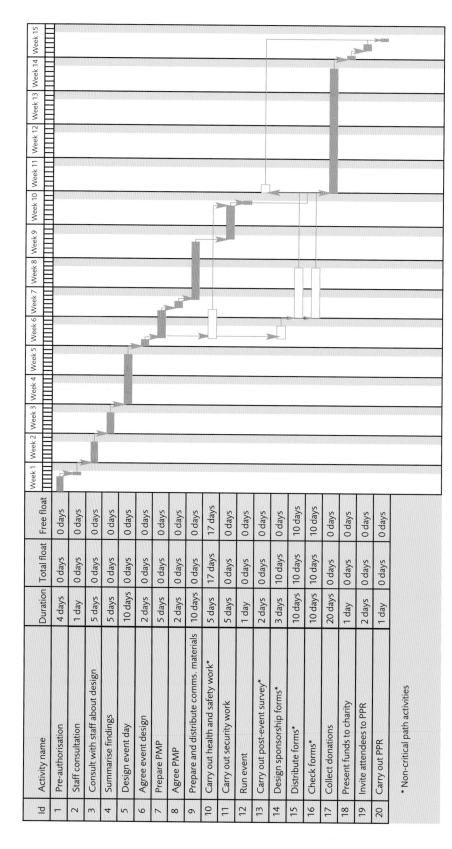

Id	Activity name	Duration	Total float	Free float
1	Pre-authorisation	4 days	0 days	0 days
2	Staff consultation	1 day	0 days	0 days
3	Consult with staff about design	5 days	0 days	0 days
4	Summarise findings	5 days	0 days	0 days
5	Design event day	10 days	0 days	0 days
6	Agree event design	2 days	0 days	0 days
7	Prepare PMP	5 days	0 days	0 days
8	Agree PMP	2 days	0 days	0 days
9	Prepare and distribute comms. materials	10 days	0 days	0 days
10	Carry out health and safety work*	5 days	17 days	17 days
11	Carry out security work	5 days	0 days	0 days
12	Run event	1 day	0 days	0 days
13	Carry out post-event survey*	2 days	0 days	0 days
14	Design sponsorship forms*	3 days	10 days	0 days
15	Distribute forms*	10 days	10 days	10 days
16	Check forms*	10 days	10 days	10 days
17	Collect donations	20 days	0 days	0 days
18	Present funds to charity	1 day	0 days	0 days
19	Invite attendees to PPR	2 days	0 days	0 days
20	Carry out PPR	1 day	0 days	0 days

* Non-critical path activities

Figure 18.3 Gantt chart showing total and free float for PCH

Milestones can also be used to set targets and monitor progress. Rather than just having a target completion date for the end of the project, interim targets based on milestones can be established that can be monitored more closely than the multitude of activities that make up the project. Many organisations also use the completion of milestones as a means of determining when they pay their suppliers or contractors. This avoids paying for work that has not been done.

A project to design and roll out a new IT system across 30 offices might have milestones planned as follows:

- User requirements completed.
- PMP signed off.
- Final design agreed.
- Pilot system tested.
- Final version agreed.
- 10 installations complete.
- 20 installations complete.
- 30 installations complete.

Project Children's Hospice (PCH)

Figure 18.3 shows the difference between total float and free float for the project.

The main milestones for the project are: (see also Figure 18.4):

- Pre-authorisation.
- Staff consultation complete.
- Event design agreed.
- Communications complete.
- PCH complete.
- Post-event survey complete.
- Funds collected.

Figure 18.4 Milestone plan for PCH

19

Resource management

First, let us clarify what we mean by resources. In project management terms, resources are the people, equipment, facilities or any other entity that is needed to complete an activity and therefore costs money. Some resources are **re-usable** (such as people) and others are **consumable** (such as concrete).

Can you think of a project where resources, specifically people with the right skills, are in unlimited supply? Most projects need to move from their ideal schedule – the one where all the work can be done to the quality you want, at the time you want and for the cost you want, to a version of the schedule that is 'realistic' and takes into account resource availability. This is generically called **resource management** but you may also hear people referring to resource optimisation. The concepts of **resource smoothing** and **resource levelling** are important because these are the ways that the project manager makes sure that the work to be done is delivered at the best possible time given the project objectives and resources available. This is another aspect of project management with particular technical language to learn, but the concepts underpinning the terms are simpler to understand than the language might suggest.

Resource management/optimisation, resource smoothing and resource levelling

Resource management is about identifying and assigning resources to activities so that the project strikes the right balance between time taken (duration) and costs in line with the project objectives and success criteria.

There is inevitably a conflict between time and cost, because no one is saying 'spend as much and take as much time as you like', so project managers need to 'optimise' resources. There are two methods used to do this.

Resource smoothing is also known as time-limited scheduling and, as the name suggests, this is the process of making sure that resources are used as efficiently as possible and of increasing or decreasing resources as required to protect the end date of the project. You would use this method when time is relatively more important than cost.

Resource levelling is also known as resource-limited scheduling and as the name suggests this is the process of making the most of the limited resources available. Resource levelling forces the amount of work scheduled not to exceed the limits of the resources available. This inevitably results in either activity durations being extended or entire activities being delayed until a resource is available. Often this means a longer overall project duration. You would use this method when cost is relatively more important than time.

One practical way of putting together the first iteration of a project schedule is to ignore the number or quantity of resources required, and the availability of these resources. The activities are sequenced and linked together graphically either using a network diagram or Gantt chart and then resources are considered as a second step to complete the picture.

In order to understand the complete picture, the resource or resources required to work on each activity must be linked to the schedule. This might be a person's name or a skill, e.g. systems analyst, lawyer, a company name, or a piece of equipment, e.g. a specialist computer, a crane or a test rig. It is important to determine the amount of each resource that is needed. Is the resource needed on a full-time or part-time basis; if it's part-time is it 10 per cent, 50 per cent or some other percentage? Once all this level of information is established and combined with the project schedule, the resources required on any given day or in any week can be seen. This kind of information is often displayed as a **resource histogram**. This is a graphical display of planned and/or actual resource usage over a period of time. It is in the form of a vertical bar chart, the height of each bar representing the quantity of resource usage in a given time unit.

Resources (and time) are often finite and problems arise when the resources required exceed the resources that are available to the project. A project manager might need five full-time data analysts for a crucial four-week period in the project, only to be told by the head of data analysis that there are only three available. In this case, what options are possible, assuming no more resources are actually available? In reality only two options exist and both will require the moving or re-scheduling of the activities that the data analysts work on. To do this the project manager will need to know if these activities have any total float and free float.

1 The first option is to try to re-schedule (in the example, the data analyst's activities), such that the need for additional resources is removed, but the end date of the project is maintained. This is the technique mentioned earlier that is known as time-limited scheduling or resource smoothing. This should always be the first thing that the project manager tries, but it doesn't always work if the activities that need to be moved are either on the critical path or have insufficient total float, the result being that the peaks either remain unchanged or are only reduced slightly.

2 Having unsuccessfully tried time-limited scheduling, the only option left is to address the peak in the most effective and least disruptive manner. But this may result in slippage of the project's end date. This technique is known as resource-limited scheduling or resource levelling. Having done this, the sponsor may be unhappy with the change to the project end date. In such a situation a discussion on how to resolve the problem will be needed.

Resource critical path/critical chain

All the information provided so far in the scheduling and resourcing sections is mainstream project thinking, and for many projects is all that is needed.

You will notice that the logical sequence of performing critical path analysis without considering resources, then adding the resources in and optimising their use does not involve fixing activities in the schedule to certain dates to 'reserve' particular people or other resources. It is bad practice to try to put together a schedule that builds in constraints that are not universally relevant, because then

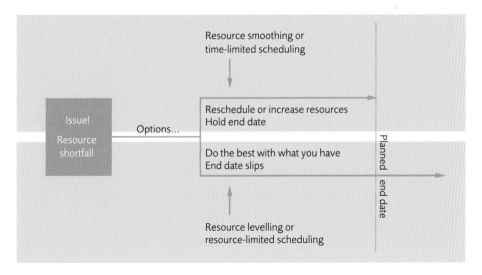

Figure19.1 Resource smoothing and leveling

the schedule does not 'flow' and becomes a picture in which the critical path cannot be truly determined.

Mainstream thinking, however, does assume that if resources are allocated to work, they will be efficient in doing that work – starting at the earliest start date and alerting the resources for the next task if they are going to finish early.

Building on his best-selling book on the *Theory of Constraints – The Goal*, Eli Goldratt challenged management thinking in 1984 by suggesting that there was a better way of performing resource optimisation than smoothing (time-limited) or levelling (resource-limited). He suggested that we should not be naïve and should reflect how people actually work, i.e. that most people tend to start a task at the latest start time not the earliest (student syndrome) and that, because most of us are multi-tasking, we are not efficient in getting work done because the 'down-time' as we juggle multiple tasks wastes time. He also noticed that because finishing a task late tends to be culturally unacceptable in our organisations, we build in hidden **contingency** or 'safety' to avoid being late, but then we squander that safety by starting at the latest start times.

Based on these observations, an alternative approach is described in Goldratt's book *Critical Chain* (1997). This book is a very important read for any aspiring project manager. In short he advocates:

1 building the schedule as normal, then
2 halving the length of each activity and building the time taken out into a buffer to protect each **critical chain** of activity
3 allocating resources to avoid multi-tasking and starting the work at the earliest start time, with hand-over as quickly as possible. Some tasks will use up some of the buffer, some will not – either needs to be OK.

Organisations that have used this approach report spectacular results on projects that are time critical. If you are starting out in project management, this approach will not be the first thing you try, but if you find yourself with a very time-sensitive project and lots of challenges with resources, maybe it's an approach you could explore further.

Other techniques that are sometimes used if time is the most important of the time/cost/quality triangle are crashing and fast-tracking.

Crashing involves reduces the estimates of effort down to their minimum level (the best case) rather than the most likely or weighted average from the PERT formula. This creates a best-case schedule that is used to incentivise the team. Delays are inevitable, but are dealt with on a case-by-case basis rather than

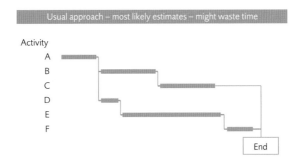

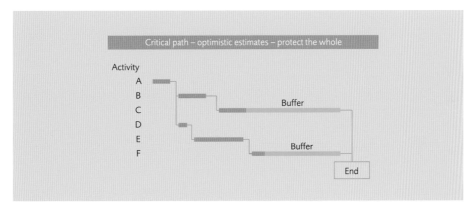

Figure 19.2 Resource critical path or critical chain

embedding what can be seen as 'padding' into the base schedule. In some ways this is a slightly cruder way of achieving what is achieved using critical chain/ resource critical path. Using crashing you run the risk of communicating to stakeholders that the 'crashed' schedule can be met, and of demotivating the team so careful communication is needed.

Fast-tracking takes different risks. In fast-tracking, the estimates of effort are not changed but the logical dependencies between activities are. An example might be that work on one part of the scope is started ahead of a dependent part of scope being finished. In an IT project, work on the coding of the system may take place before the final requirements and specifications have been formally signed off. This can save time if all goes well, but results in re-work if the calculated risk backfires.

All scheduling and resource management activities, however, rely on a complete definition of scope, a good understanding of logical dependencies and informed estimates of effort from the available resources.

Project Children's Hospice (PCH)

You are quite lucky because the project has very few resource issues. However, you have recognised during Week 6 of the project that you yourself are working on two activities 'prepare PMP' and 'design sponsorship forms'. You have estimated that you will need to spend 75 per cent of your time on each of these. If this estimate proves true, then you will be overloaded. In order to avoid this, you should consider re-scheduling the work relating to designing sponsorship forms. Moving this work one week, i.e. within its total float, should solve your resourcing problem.

For this project, resource-limited scheduling is not possible due to the immovable end date. If resource constraints became impossible to manage, the options would be to either:

- find more resources by agreeing more company time or by securing extra funding for outside help, or
- reduce the scope of the project so less work is done.

20

Procurement

Not all projects need procurement. Sometimes all the resources that a project needs can be found 'in-house'. Usually though, the project team will need to procure (buy) services or goods from third-party suppliers. This section therefore explores why projects need a procurement strategy/plan as part of the PMP to guide decisions on what to buy, which suppliers to choose and the best ways to form contracts with suppliers.

You might wonder why a specific procurement plan is needed. We obviously procure things all the time when we buy our groceries at the supermarket, purchase books or music on the internet or take a taxi ride. We may not do this very formally because we don't need to. Projects are different. For one thing we are usually spending someone else's money, perhaps lots of it, and things must be delivered on time and to the right quality. The margin for error is usually less and the risks are usually higher, therefore we need to think through actions more carefully. On a very large project, there may be a whole department of procurement specialists to support the project manager. Where this is the case though, the project manager remains responsible for delivering the project to its objectives. The procurement specialists are providing an internal service as part of the project team.

Procurement

Procurement is defined as the securing of goods and services. There are other words that are often used synonymously with procurement including: purchasing, as in the purchasing of materials or equipment (goods) and contracting, as in the contracting of personnel or an organisation (services).

The purpose of a procurement strategy/plan

In projects where lots of procurement needs to be done it is important to define a **procurement strategy/plan**. This will set out how goods and services

Resource	Needed	Available	Shortfall
Analysts	2	2	
Programmers	10	5	Procure from suppliers to secure resources
Trainers	2	1	
Testers	6	2	
Computers	10	10	
Room	1	1	

Figure 20.1 Project procurement process

will be acquired for the project. This part of the PMP needs to consider such factors as:

- whether to **make or buy** what is needed, e.g. whether to design the software system from scratch or buy a ready-made system
- use of a single integrated supplier or multiple discrete suppliers, e.g. using one builder to do all the building works and be responsible for plumbing, electrical work and decorating or use separate suppliers managed by yourself
- how suppliers will be selected, what form of contract will be used, will you have a competitive tender, what legal jurisdiction will you contract within, and how suppliers will be paid, e.g. will you pay against milestones or only upon completion
- you also need to consider if you want suppliers to be remunerated based on a lump sum/**fixed price** or on some form of reimbursable basis.

It is the project manager's responsibility to ensure that certain key principles are followed when selecting and managing contractors and suppliers. These principles are designed to enable fair and amicable working arrangements between the two parties, i.e. the company or organisation and the contractor or supplier. Listed below are some of the key principles that a project manager should follow:

1 Use an objective process when selecting a contractor or supplier to avoid the influence of personal preferences, or worse – practices that could be construed as bribery (this would be part of the procurement strategy/plan if one has been prepared).
2 Make sure there is understanding of what your organisation wants from the arrangement.
3 Make sure there is understanding of what the contractor or supplier wants from the arrangement.
4 Check out whether the contractor or supplier is really able to do the work that is required, to the required time, cost and quality objectives.
5 Be clear about who is taking what risks as part of the contractual arrangements.
6 Involve the contractor or supplier in project team activities wherever practicable to do so.

There is much recent research and development to improve the way that project supply chains actually work. There is a general trend of moving away from adversarial relationships and an attempt to transfer risk in the supply chain and moving towards mutually beneficial 'win–win' contracts, where risk is shared on a pain/gain share basis. Projects work best when there is collaboration between clients and contractors in the supply chain and where each party is incentivised to keep communication channels open and to work together to achieve the objectives. Remember, risk can be priced, but cannot be sold!

In projects where there are multiple suppliers performing key aspects of the work there are a number of ways of working with the supply chain. Some organisations prefer to have a prime contractor, often referred to as 'one throat to choke', with all other suppliers reporting through the prime. This, on the face of it, makes it easier for the client organisation, but the reality can be different if the prime and their sub-contractors do not have 'fair' or aligned contractual terms and/or good working relationships. The client keeps more control by having all the contractors reporting to them and taking a more active role in building the team of in-house and contract resources to deliver the project.

All of the considerations above need to be resolved and the chosen approach documented in the project management plan.

Supplier remuneration (paying suppliers)

Another key consideration is the method of remuneration that the project uses. This can be a complicated area, but in short there are three basic forms of remuneration:

1 **Reimbursable** – the supplier is paid an agreed rate for all the time and all the materials they expend on the project (hence the term 'time and materials' is often used).
2 **Fixed price (often called lump sum)** – the supplier is paid an agreed total amount for a defined scope, perhaps with milestone payments for interim deliverables.
3 *Partnering contract* – the client and supplier(s) agree a target price and then share the pain if this is not achieved, or the gain if it is.

Variations on all these reimbursement methods exist – it is a specialist area and you will have procurement experts in your organisation to help you – but hopefully you can see that the form of contract drives different behaviours and introduces different risks to be managed within the project.

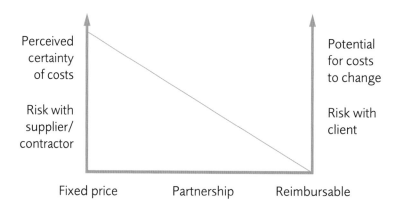

Figure 20.2 Ways of paying suppliers

Project Children's Hospice (PCH)

You only have £500 of the company's money to spend on the project unless you can persuade the sponsor to let you spend more or can find alternative sources of income. With such a small amount to spend, you are unlikely to want to place any contracts, but you are likely to purchase materials and services for promotion and communications. You are also considering purchasing T-shirts emblazoned with your company's logo and the children's hospice logo for all event organisers to wear.

Your procurement strategy for such a simple procurement activity doesn't have to consider many options. For obvious reasons you have no choice over whether to make or buy the T-shirts and it would be pointless going to more than one supplier. You would almost certainly ask a number of suppliers to give you a quote; you might even be able to do a good deal as the T-shirts are for a charitable event. Regarding payment, it is likely that your supplier will require a large percentage or full payment with the order so again there is little to consider.

21

Budgeting

Once the project manager has pulled together information on scope and requirements, schedule, resources, risk and procurement, they can then create the cost plan or budget for the project, i.e. what money will need to be spent and when.

The management of cost throughout the life cycle (cost management and cost control) is covered in Chapter 26. This chapter covers only the creation of the initial budget as the final planning step before review, approval and baselining of the project management plan (PMP).

Creating a budget

A mistake that some people make when putting together the budget for the project is to disconnect this from the rest of the planning work. Hopefully you can see that a spreadsheet or other table that says how much money the project is forecasted to spend each month must be derived from a resourced schedule. This is often called the **planned cost (PC)** or the budgeted cost of work scheduled (BCWS).

To create the project budget, the project manager needs to look at the time periods ahead (typically month by month, but could be weekly, daily or quarterly depending on the project) and to determine what work is planned in that period.

The resourced schedule will provide the effort from the people who have been allocated and using agreed hourly rates, the cost of the 'labour' element of the project can be built up. Often, the costs of **sub-contract** labour are not built up in detail because the contractor has a fixed-price contract, so they have to provide as much labour as needed to meet the agreed timescales. In this case, contract costs will be built up over time according to the contract. The project may only incur **actual cost** when a milestone payment is made to the contractor, but costs will have accrued between those periods.

Once in-house and contract labour costs have been planned, the project manager can then look at other costs – for materials and other services.

If the project manager has built a completely resourced schedule, then estimates for materials will be included, for example, how many bricks are needed and when, or when new hardware that is needed to support development of software will be bought. This doesn't happen in the schedule in less mature organisations though, so the budgeted costs of such items will be entered straight into the budgeting spreadsheet or table.

Cost contingency

The final point to make about budgeting is about cost contingency. It is usual for organisations to include a contingency to cover unforeseen costs not already included in their estimated cost. The simplest and least accurate way of doing this is to add a percentage depending on the perceived risk in the plan. The most thorough way of doing this is to build up the contingency figure by looking at the combined effects of estimating uncertainty and the risks identified in the risk log. Some organisations will hold contingency at two different levels. A contingency figure that is allocated to the project manager to manage estimating uncertainty and identified risks and an additional **management reserve** held by the project sponsor to deal with emerging risk.

Most organisations will also have financial guidance for how to deal with exchange rates, inflation and other variables that could change the actual cost of the project but are out of the project manager's control.

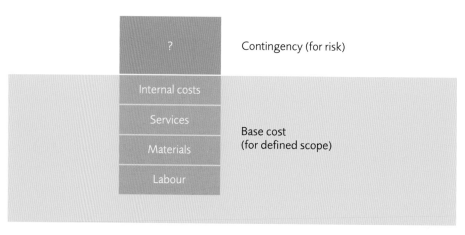

Figure 21.1 Base costs plus contingency

Project Children's Hospice (PCH)

It has been made clear to you that your financial budget has an absolute ceiling of £500. However, you have decided to prepare a budget based on 1,000 hours of involvement agreed with the sponsor. Your time is budgeted at 550 hours effort. Each games manager should spend no more than 100 hours. You have budgeted 50 hours for health and safety, and 10 hours each for finance and quality. The remaining 80 hours will be held as contingency for the time being.

22

The project management plan

All the way through this section on the Definition (planning) phase of the project life cycle we have referred to the project management plan, or PMP. This is the key management product that must be created by the project manager in this phase. All the different plans that form the PMP are brought together and baselined as part of the approvals to continue into the next phase of the life cycle. They need to form a coherent whole, a document that takes forward the business case produced in the first life cycle phase to further define the Why for the project, and then go on to describe What, When, Who and How Much for the project.

What is the PMP?

The PMP does not need to be a big or complicated document, but it must outline the way in which the project will be taken forward in a way that all stakeholders can understand.

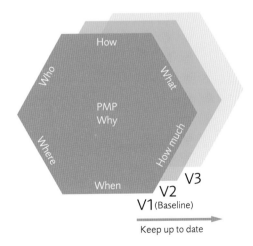

Figure 22.1 Purpose and content of the project management plan (PMP)

You may often hear people refer to the 'PID' for their project. This usually means the project initiation document. In the PRINCE2® methodology for projects, the PID is equivalent to the PMP.

As previously mentioned, when the project manager has approval from the sponsor and any project board or steering group to proceed from the Definition (planning) phase of the project, the contents of the PMP are then baselined, which means that any changes must be made through change control. More details about change control are included in Chapter 24. It is the project manager's job to make sure that the PMP is up to date and that all the project team agree that it is a valid plan for delivering the project.

Why have a PMP?

The benefits of defining the PMP and keeping it up to date are primarily related to clarity of information. With a PMP in place, at any point in time team members will

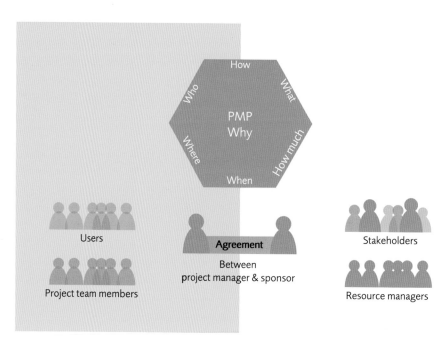

Figure 22.2 Agreeing the PMP

have all the information they need to understand the project and the work they need to do. This is particularly useful when things change, for example, if there is a new member of the team. Another way of considering the PMP is as the contract between the project manager and their team and the sponsor. In this way the PMP is clearly a response to the business case and everyone is clear about all aspects of how the project will meet the success criteria.

Project Children's Hospice (PCH)

Before starting your project it would be wise to consider and document the following:

Why you are carrying out the project?	Because it is in support of a local charity that you feel strongly about. It will also be a very good social event for the company.
How you will do it?	By running a fundraising event at work on the designated day.
What you are going to do?	Consult with staff, design the games to take place, communicate, run the 'day' itself and collect donations.
How much will it cost?	There will be no more than £500 external expenditure but company resources, such as photocopy consumables, will be used for free. It will also require no more than 1,000 hours of staff time, which is being donated at no charge to the project.
When you are going to do the work?	Over the next 10 weeks, meeting a number of milestones on the way.
Where you are going to do it?	Wholly within the company head office.
Who will do the work?	You and other corporate resources including legal, reprographics and HR.

The points in the table cover the major components of a PMP. It should be obvious why it is best to consider each of these points before spending any money or a lot of time on the project. It would be far better to know before you start if you cannot have free access to photocopier consumables so that you can make alternative arrangements. The PMP needs further work before it is a working plan that can be formally agreed between you and the sponsor, but this is a start.

You are accountable for the project management plan (PMP) for the project. Only if the document you prepare, in whatever format, is read and understood by all those involved (primarily your project team, including the sponsor) can you avoid disagreements later when they claim not to understand what you intended to do, when you intended to do it and the assistance you needed from them.

The development (execution) phase

Introduction

In this section we look at the third phase of the project life cycle, the Development phase. It is during this phase that the project management plan (PMP) is executed, monitored, controlled and, when necessary and agreed, updated.

A number of the topics included in this section are closely related. Issues, or problems the project manager cannot solve alone are closely linked to change control, which itself ties in closely with **configuration management**.

Issue management recognises that there are things that a project manager needs help in managing. Appropriate **escalation** of problems (issues) should be seen as strong management, not weak management. The occurrence of issues is one source of **project change**. All **change requests** need to go through formal change control in order to avoid scope creep and the inevitable failure to meet time, cost and quality objectives and stakeholder expectations when this happens.

The process of configuration management is required to ensure that after a change has been made all the 'knock-on' effects are understood and managed. Failure to do this will inevitably lead to some other failure in the future – when a part of the solution is out of date.

Two other topics that are included in the Development phase are monitoring and control, and information management and reporting. Again these two are closely linked. Monitoring tells us where we are on a project. If monitoring tells us we are not on track, control attempts to adjust the project to recover the situation as well as possible. In order to monitor (and control), the project needs to capture and report accurate and timely progress-related information. Information is also needed to inform and manage the expectations of key project stakeholders. Progress information is only one type of information that needs to be captured as part of an information management system. All information generated on a project needs to be captured, stored and protected in a planned manner.

Figure 23.1 Development (execution) phase – overview

23

Issue management

The word issue is used in a very specific way in project management. During the life of the project problems will arise and the project manager has to deal with them. Some of these problems will be easily dealt with, while others will need support from the sponsor and other stakeholders before they can be resolved. Problems that fall into this latter category are called issues and are subject to issue management to remove the threats they pose.

Issues and issue management

Historically issues have been considered to be problems or concerns that exist today, that will affect project objectives if not resolved but where the project manager cannot resolve the situation alone. However, some people use a more theoretical definition of an issue that relates to **tolerances** for delegated authority being exceeded. While this is a valid extension of how some organisations interpret issues, it is an unnecessary complication when starting out in project management.

When issues are identified it is good practice for the project manager to capture them in an **issue log** (sometimes called an issue register) so that they are not forgotten, a resolution is always obtained and there is a record of the things that happened and decisions taken in response. This is issue management.

Issues and risks

Hopefully it is obvious that issues and risks are different, although related. Issues are things that have happened, whereas risks are things that might happen. Risks may materialise into issues. Issues may be causes of new risks. Both need to be managed.

Examples of issues might be:

- Two of our key resources have left the company.
- The prototype has failed all its initial tests.
- Joe and Jane find it impossible to work together but they are both essential project resources.
- There are no suppliers that can meet our specification requirements.
- Prices received from bidders are at least twice what we estimated.

You can see from this list of example issues that some of them regard people directly, such as Joe and Jane's difficulties in working together, while others are problems about deliverables, such as the prototype that failed initial tests. Although it is not always true that an unresolved issue will result in a conflict between people, it is often true. It follows then that one of the purposes of issue management is to prevent problems and concerns becoming crises for the project. Resolving conflicts between stakeholders and/or project team members requires special skills, takes time and costs money that could otherwise be put to better use.

Some people might say that resolving issues is just part of a manager's job, so why add bureaucracy by logging issues and monitoring them formally? There are three responses to this point. First, issues as described are not just any problem that needs resolution. If the project manager can sort it out themselves, then they should just get on with that. Only if the problem would cause a significant impact on the project if it wasn't resolved *and* the project manager cannot resolve it alone should an issue be raised.

Second, using an issue log means that issues are not forgotten and resources are allocated to see the issue through to a conclusion. In the same way that risks should be allocated a risk owner, issues should be allocated an issue owner – the person best placed to resolve the issue on behalf of the project manager.

Third, logging issues provides traceability of decisions made. This third point is particularly important because there is a direct connection between issues,

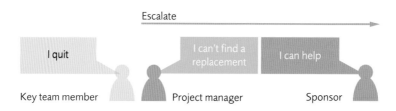

Figure 23.2 Escalate to resolve issues

project changes and hence change control. Change control is a process that ensures that all requests to change the baseline scope and plans of a project, are captured, evaluated and then approved/rejected/deferred, and implemented if approved. We will discuss this further in the next chapter but hopefully it is clear that many change requests will arise as a direct result of an issue.

Project Children's Hospice (PCH)

It is traditional in your company that on one Friday every year a large proportion of staff take time off to play in an inter-departmental golf match. You have just been made aware that the date being discussed for this is the same day as PCH is planned. Obviously PCH cannot change, therefore you have an issue that needs resolving. There is no way that you can instruct the golf match organisers to change their date. As both your boss and the managing director are invited to participate in the golf match, you feel that by escalating the issue to them it may get some attention.

24

Change control

Change control is the process that the project manager implements to make sure that the business case and PMP remain up to date through the phases of the project life cycle. The process starts from the point where a change is requested, often verbally. It progresses through a decision-making stage about whether to implement the change or not, and concludes with communication and documentation of the results of the decision. Change control can seem an overly bureaucratic process at first glance, but those who have experienced the impact of un-managed project changes have come to appreciate the process the hard way.

Project change and the use of a change request

A project is the means by which new products, services or improvements are developed and introduced in a controlled way. All projects start off with defined time, cost, quality objectives and other success criteria, linked to the scope of work that will achieve them. In an ideal world, these parameters would remain constant. We don't live in an ideal world and, as a result, it is very unlikely that the objectives and scope of the project will remain constant throughout the project life cycle. Project changes will occur, and when they do, it will probably be for one of the following reasons:

- a change in justification for the project
- a change in requirements to the scope or specification of deliverables, perhaps due to a change in legislation or regulation
- the discovery of a mistake or error such that the delivered outputs will no longer work
- an incorrect estimate of time or money
- a reduction in resource availability
- a technological or market place change.

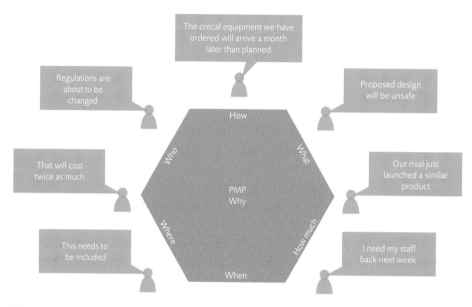

Figure 24.1 Many things lead to a change

The result of any of the above will trigger a **change request**. A change request may arise through changes in the business or issues affecting the project. Because such requests will inevitably change the plans for the project, and often the business case too, they must be taken seriously and evaluated systematically.

It is important to note the use of the word request. A change *request* is just that – it is not an order to change (although some stakeholders will be more influential than others and will need a very good justification if the request is to be rejected). The request is the trigger for a change to be formally considered.

Change freeze

Some organisations openly adopt a **change freeze**, or no-change mentality, after a particular phase in the project life cycle, typically after Definition. This is done both to discourage changes, which will have a disruptive effect on the project and be costly to implement, and also to emphasise the need to get an agreed set of requirements 'up front' such that the complete project scope can be defined. The only time that changes are allowed is when the

158

deliverables would be unsafe, not work or be in contradiction of a legal or regulatory requirement.

Project change control

One of the key responsibilities of a project manager during the Development phase of the project is the application and administration of formal change control.

Project change control is a means by which project change requests are captured, evaluated, approved and implemented. Without this process, there would be a 'free for all', with perhaps those who shouted the loudest being the ones to get what they want. This is not the best scenario for the project as a whole. Without formal change control the project's scope is likely to creep (gradually increase) and, as a result, the cost will increase and probably the end date will slip.

If you are a project manager it is inevitable that you will get informal requests to make changes on a project, e.g. you might be asked to purchase some new desktop computers as part of the roll-out of the new IT system. Even though you might think that it is the right thing to do to buy the new computers, and there is enough money in the budget to do so, this request, like all other change requests, should be subjected to formal change control. Only if this is done might you become aware that there is another project in progress that will replace all desktop computers with laptops.

Formal change control is the method that ensures that the project plans are kept up-to-date throughout the project life cycle.

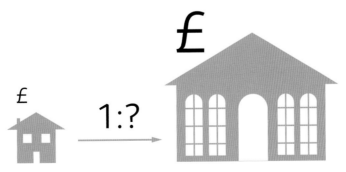

Figure 24.2 If only we had used formal change control

The steps involved in a change control process and the use of the change log (register)

A formal change control process should be applied on all projects. Formal change control encompasses four main steps: capturing or recording of the proposed change, evaluation or impact assessment, approval (or not) and implementation.

Proposed project changes are usually documented on a change request form and then captured or recorded in a **change log** (change register means exactly the same thing). All changes need to be recorded in the change log. The change log lists all project changes whatever their status: proposed, approved, rejected or deferred. A change log is often no more than a table created in word-processing software, or a spreadsheet or database, that lists key aspects of a change. These will include:

- a unique number for the change
- who requested it
- a description of the change request
- impact assessment:
    - time
    - cost
    - quality
    - other success criteria
    - risk
    - stakeholder expectations
- cumulative effect on objectives
- status of the change (accepted, rejected or deferred)
- date when a decision was made.

Most project managers find keeping the change log up-to-date an invaluable aid both during the project and at the end of it. During the project it will help in understanding the changes that are in the pipeline and their potential impact on the project. At the end of the project it will allow the project manager to explain, if explanation is needed, why the project cost more or less than planned, took a longer or shorter time than planned or why the quality of the deliverables varied from the plan.

As you can see from the list of items in the change log, once logged, the change is then subjected to a review, which will include an impact assessment. The results of this impact assessment are included on both the change request form and in the change log. The assessed changed should then be submitted to the appropriate authority who will do one of three things: approve the change, reject it, or defer it. Typical authorities might be the sponsor, or a change control board, or in some cases the project manager may authorise changes to a certain limit.

Whichever response is made, the person who requested the change should be informed of the decision. Changes that are approved must then be implemented, and this will include updating the overall project management plan (PMP) and any associated and detailed documentation, such as the project schedule and the budget.

For example, as the project manager for a new computer system, you may receive a change request from one of the key users for more functionality. Even though they might have a very compelling argument why this change needs to be implemented, you must still apply change control. After logging the changes, all the consequences of its impact must be assessed, including

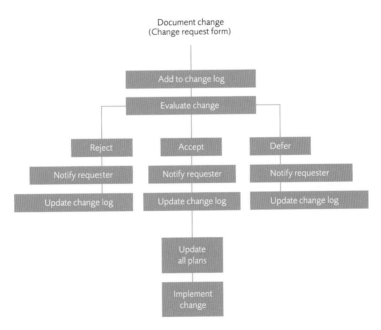

Figure 24.3 A change control process

doing nothing. If, after assessment of the change, the decision is to reject it, then it is your responsibility to communicate this to the user who requested the change. If the decision is to approve it, then you must re-work all the project plans accordingly.

Project Children's Hospice (PCH)

The company's managing director has just bumped into you in the corridor and asked you what would be the effect on the project if you were to arrange six games on the day rather than three as planned. He was very keen to point out that this was not an instruction, but this does amount to being a change request.

Your managing director could have adopted a more forceful approach when requesting the change. He could have said that you were to ignore any change control process and 'just do it'. If you had chosen to take this approach, there is a good chance that when the project was over it would become apparent that the 1,000 hours budget of staff time specified as a constraint was exceeded. It is also quite likely that your boss (the sponsor) would not be too pleased about this, so the 'just do it' approach must be avoided even if the change process used to agree changed plans is relatively informal.

You have just found out that the reason why the managing director has requested a change is because there is an issue. It needs resolving and a project change might be one of the ways to do it. The issue is that a number of staff are feeling left out of the fun. They feel that only three games will prevent them from actively participating. As a result, some staff are becoming quite anti the whole thing. This is the last thing you or the company want. You cannot resolve this issue yourself, but it looks like your MD may have pre-empted the problem and is trying to assist in its resolution by requesting a change.

The process you are informally adopting is a good example of a change control process. You have received notification of a change request that you would be wise to confirm in writing, perhaps via email. Assuming you are running a change log, you will have registered the change request in it. The impact assessment you have carried out should be documented, along with the reason for the change, and submitted to the sponsor for approval or rejection (deferral is not an option here).

If the sponsor approves the change, you must update the project objectives and plans accordingly and notify all those involved of the changes. If the sponsor rejects the change, you must inform the requestor (the managing director) that this is the case and find another way of handling the project issue about the involvement of staff and their commitment to the project.

25

Configuration management

In many ways configuration management is just a more complex way of saying version control. The official definition of the term configuration as detailed in the glossary is 'the set of functional and physical characteristics of a final deliverable defined in specification and achieved in the execution of plans'. This is a grand definition but the practicalities are simple. Managing the configuration actually means making sure that all the pieces of the project 'jigsaw' can be identified, that they fit together and that they are documented in a way such that replacement pieces could be made if it became necessary. In some ways configuration management is closely related to specifications as part of project quality management (Chapter 14). In other ways it is closely related to change control (Chapter 24) because any approved change will affect the configuration.

Configuration identification and configuration control

Configuration is the word used to describe the sum of the different items (elements) of the project that need to be controlled. Some of these elements might be physical things such as a component of a bridge, some elements might be software code and others will be documents or drawings. Each different element is called a configuration item and must be identified through configuration identification. Configuration items must have a unique identification, a specific purpose and they must all be controlled through configuration management.

Configuration management is the administrative work that needs to be done to create unique identities for configuration items and to control changes as they occur. Configuration management is the responsibility of the project manager.

While some people relate to configuration management as version control, others say that configuration management is best described as very detailed change control. Change control and configuration management are necessarily

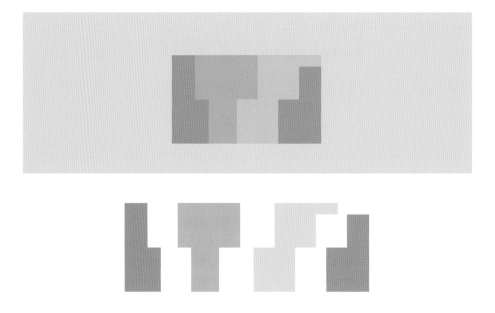

Figure 25.1 Configuration items

linked because an authorised project change always results in at least one configuration item needing to be updated.

For example, in a project to install new signage across a company, a configuration item would be the company's logo and another would be the font to be used. If anything changed on the logo or the font during the life of the project, this would obviously have a significant impact on all the signage.

Another example is the control of drawings on any design project. Each drawing is itself a configuration item. Any change in any drawing will need to be reflected in any other affected drawings and also in other areas like sizes of materials or equipment. In this example, as in many others, configuration management tends to be seen as document or version control.

If a problem during project development arises, the project manager will need to refer back to the previous specifications of each configuration item. Traceability for accounting purposes, and accountability for communication with stakeholders, are both key parts of configuration management and are achieved with the help of accurate, up-to-date and securely held documentation.

If the example of design drawings is considered again, then suitable documentation in this case would be a register of some description that recorded the following:

- the title of the drawing, with a unique identification code or number (the configuration item)
- a revision or version number
- its current approval status.

This kind of documentation needs to be in place for each configuration item. It is also essential that, from a 'top-down' perspective, there is a clear picture of how each individual configuration item affects other items. For example, if a logo is a configuration item, which other items would need to be changed if the logo had to change?

In many organisations a configuration librarian role exists as part of the project management office (PMO) or quality department to maintain records for the whole configuration. Such a role maintains a document that shows the current version of each configuration item. Where such support is not in place, the project manager must do the work themself.

Why use configuration management?

The most fundamental point is that configuration management is a way of maintaining control of the constituent parts of the project. Changes at all levels must be subjected to configuration control so that each configuration item's status can be controlled and logged. This means that, at any point in time, all the project team can recognise the current version of any item. Working, in any way, on superseded items must be avoided.

Unique identifier	Version	Status	Used on
AAA	1	Superseded	ABC, AFQ
AAA	2	Current	ABC, AFQ
AAB	1	Current	AAA, CAB
AAC	1	Current	ZYW, XFG
etc.			

Figure 25.2 Configuration item status

The importance of configuration management in certain industries cannot be understated. There have been numerous documented catastrophes that have been caused due to errors in configuration management, including a failed mission to the planet Mars and French trains that were built too wide for the platforms. As a result, configuration management is subject to close verification and audit throughout the project life cycle.

Project Children's Hospice (PCH)

One of the configuration items that you have identified for the project is the name of the celebrity who will pay a visit to your company on the day of the event. The celebrity's name will be used on all communication media. You have promised to introduce all participants to her, and you need to plan accordingly. As you can see, if the celebrity was changed, it would have a considerable knock-on effect throughout the rest of the project.

Another configuration item is the children's hospice charity logo. You may be pretty certain that it isn't going to change in the next 10 weeks, but it would make sense to confirm for sure that you are using the correct version and are not contravening any house style in your written and web-based communications.

26

Monitoring and control

Once a project is being worked on it is essential to know how well things are going. The ways in which this is done is brought together under the heading of monitoring and control. Monitoring is the action of checking how things are going so you can know the status of the project in terms of the schedule, budget, quality and other success criteria. Once you know the status, if you are not on track, control is doing something about it.

Monitoring

During the Definition phase of the project, the project management plan is put in place and baselined. As we have already outlined, the PMP includes:

- definition of scope and quality requirements
- a resourced schedule
- a budget
- other plans for stakeholder engagement/communication, procurement and risk management.

Progress against each of these is monitored on a periodic basis. Are deliverables meeting quality requirements, and if not, why not? Is re-work taking place adding time and cost to the project? Is the project ahead of or behind schedule? Are individual activities ahead of or behind schedule? Are resources being provided on time? If progress continues at the same rate, will the project finish early, on time or late? Likewise, similar questions can be asked against the budget. Is the project underspending or overspending? If the rate of spend continues in relation to the work being done, will the project finish under budget, on budget or over budget? Are stakeholders happy? Are contractors happy? What is the current risk profile? Are risks being managed?

How often project progress is measured will depend on many factors including the complexity, duration, budget of the project and stakeholder needs. For many projects it is quite sufficient to monitor progress on a monthly basis. For other

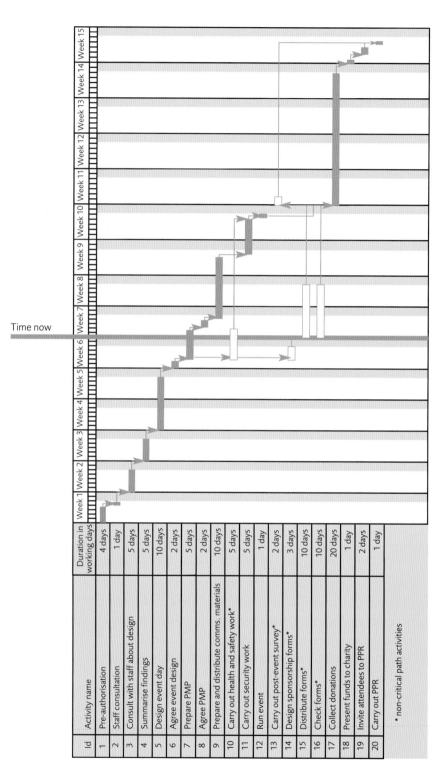

Id	Activity name	Duration in working days
1	Pre-authorisation	4 days
2	Staff consultation	1 day
3	Consult with staff about design	5 days
4	Summarise findings	5 days
5	Design event day	10 days
6	Agree event design	2 days
7	Prepare PMP	5 days
8	Agree PMP	2 days
9	Prepare and distribute comms. materials	10 days
10	Carry out health and safety work*	5 days
11	Carry out security work	5 days
12	Run event	1 day
13	Carry out post-event survey*	2 days
14	Design sponsorship forms*	3 days
15	Distribute forms*	10 days
16	Check forms*	10 days
17	Collect donations	20 days
18	Present funds to charity	1 day
19	Invite attendees to PPR	2 days
20	Carry out PPR	1 day

* non-critical path activities

Time now

Week 1 Week 2 Week 3 Week 4 Week 5 Week 6 Week 7 Week 8 Week 9 Week 10 Week 11 Week 12 Week 13 Week 14 Week 15

Figure 26.1 Gantt chart showing progress for PCH

projects, or at key times in projects, progress will need to be monitored daily, or even hourly.

In addition to 'normal' progress monitoring the governance for the project may demand more formal reviews at key points in the life cycle. While these reviews often fall at the end of a phase and can be called gate reviews, they can also be at other significant milestones during a phase – perhaps prior to awarding a major contract or when there is going to be a handover between departments or functions.

Project Children's Hospice (PCH)

The project is currently on schedule. All critical path activities have either been completed on time or are in progress. However, Activities 10 and 14 have not started on time. Because Activity 10 has free float, no subsequent activities have been delayed (so far). The delay in Activity 14 will cause a delay in the start of Activities 15 and 16. This will not delay the project at this point in time, again because of free float, but this needs to be managed closely.

Earned value management

One technique for monitoring project progress that is used extensively in some industries is **earned value management (EVM)**. While this might sound complicated, in its basic form it is actually quite simple. The difference between EVM and simpler monitoring approaches is the recognition that the money you spend or the amount of resources used are not necessarily indicative of the amount of work completed. Put another way, the fact that you have spent 50 per cent of the budget or used half of the allocated resource effort doesn't mean you have done half the work and therefore the project is 50 per cent complete. In fact, the picture could be very different. You could have spent half the budget but the work cost more than estimated, meaning you are overspending, or conversely the work could have been done cheaper or more efficiently and you are underspending. All combinations are possible.

In order to make earned value management work you need to know three things:

- planned cost (or the budgeted cost of work scheduled)
- actual cost (or the actual cost of work performed)
- **earned value** (the budgeted cost of work performed).

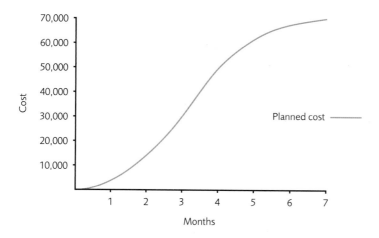

Figure 26.2 Example of earned value management – planned cost curve

Planned cost is the money you planned to spend on the work for the project (the budget for the agreed scope). This planned cost needs to be phased over the duration of the project showing when the money would be spent. If you show this on a graph it normally depicts some sort of 'S' shape or **'S' curve** (see Figure 26.2). What you have created here is your planned cost/expenditure curve for the project.

Actual cost is what you are actually spending over time. This can be picked up from timesheets, anticipated invoices or via an internal finance system. Note this actual expenditure is not related to cashflow but to when money is due to be paid (financial accruals). You can then compare what has been spent to what you planned to spend (see Figure 26.3). Unfortunately, as explained earlier, this doesn't really tell you how you are doing on the project; there is one component missing – earned value.

Earned value relates to the budgeted (intended) cost for the work you have actually performed. With this final ingredient it is possible to make some appropriate comparisons of the three pieces of information, planned cost (PC), actual cost (AC) and earned value (EV).

Figure 26.4 shows a planned cost curve for a project that is scheduled to take seven months and with a budget of £70,000 (noted this could be 700,000 hours). At the end of month three, the planned budget was £30,000, the actual cost was £40,000 and the earned value £20,000. What this tells us is that, at this point in time, the project has completed £10,000 worth of work less than planned and the

172

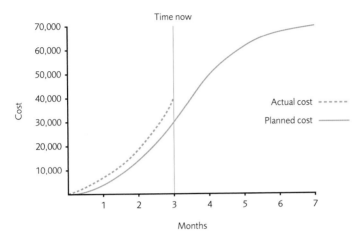

Figure 26.3 Example of earned value management – with actual costs

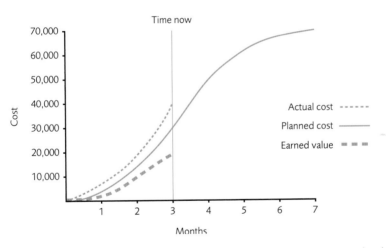

Figure 26.4 Example of earned value management – earned value

work has actually cost £20,000 more than was budgeted for. If this rate or lack of progress continues, the project will not only finish over budget but it will also be late. There are some formulas that can be used to work out the productivity and efficiency of the project to date so that the expected completion date and **estimate at completion** (out-turn cost) can be projected (assuming progress continues on the same trajectory). This is quite complicated for people who are starting out in project management, but it is worth looking out for further reading on this if earned value management is used in your organisation.

Control

Knowing where you are in terms of progress on a project is obviously very important, but just being able to say that you are behind or ahead of schedule or that you are over or under spending is not enough. What is important is doing something about it. While it is not always possible to rectify the situation, sometimes this can be achieved by:

- re-planning the project, re-sequencing activities or re-prioritising work
- allocating more or better resources to activities (note this may improve the schedule but will increase costs)
- outsourcing the work to others (this would almost certainly increase costs)
- adjusting the quality to make things cheaper and potentially easier to do (this could impact the reliability of the deliverables)
- reducing the scope to allow the work to be completed on time and within budget (this may have side-effects in respect of performance and meeting benefits).

None of the above controlling actions can be taken without a clear understanding of the project's business case and where priorities lie. Is it more important to finish on time than on budget or vice versa? Is delivering the complete scope to the agreed quality more important than both time and cost, and therefore can a schedule slippage and cost overrun be tolerated (at least to some degree)?

Cost control and cost management

One distinct aspect of monitoring and control that warrants further attention relates to the tracking of project costs. In the earlier section on earned value the term accrual was mentioned; this is just one of the terms that we need to consider here. These are the others, all of which are relevant to cost control and cost management:

- **Commitment** – the amount of money that relates to the placement of an order or contract that effectively is spent once the deal has been done. It is money that you will have to pay at some time in the future when work has been done. It is possible to have committed almost all of a project's budget within days of the start if one big contract has been placed with a supplier to do all the work.

- **Accrual** – the amount of money that relates to work done for which payment is due but has not actually been made. This can often happen when suppliers are late in submitting invoices or when invoices take time to be processed within an organisation. Once money has been accrued it cannot be spent on anything else.
- **Actual money paid out** – the money that has actually left the company's bank account.

By understanding what money has been paid out and what accruals there are, the project can then say what its actual expenditure (actual cost) is at any point in time. Understanding this, the total commitments and the remaining work to be done will allow the project manager to forecast the final out-turn cost of the project or the estimate at completion.

27

Information management and reporting

Effective **information management** enables project teams to use their time, resources and expertise effectively to make decisions and to fulfil their roles. The role of information management is to turn the vast amount of data generated by a project into information, often in the form of reports. Therefore, in this chapter, we have also included project reporting, which closely relates to the previous chapter on monitoring and control, as well as Chapter 10 on communication.

Information management

The process of information management encompasses the collection, storage, distribution, archiving and (eventual) appropriate destruction of project information.

Collection: Project information can take many forms: written, video, oral, audio and electronic. Two important guidelines are: collect only as much information as reasonably needed (remember turning data into information mentioned above); and assure its quality, i.e. that it can be trusted. It is not difficult to imagine the serious consequences that can arise from the violation of either guideline. Having collected the information, it must be appropriately classified or categorised in order to make it useful in the future.

Storage: Information must be stored for a range of purposes including: analysis, identifying historical trends, developing **lessons learned**, satisfying legislative requirements etc. Appropriate controls – including user access, export controls, versioning, change control, audit, and back-ups – must be established. Where required, different security arrangements may need to be put in place according to the security classification of the relevant information.

Dissemination: Information is only useful if it can be used to manage the current project or for future benefit to the organisation. Consequently, information dissemination involves consideration of questions such as: what information is to be distributed, to whom, in what format, how often, under what circumstances and using what security protocols? You may recognise a lot of this as part of the communication plan.

Archiving: After a period of time, usually determined by a mix of company policy and judgement, information is often archived. When most information was paper-based this meant sending it to large-scale storage repositories that can take time to access. Information is archived for a diverse range of purposes, including regulatory, e.g. quality test records, historical, future benchmarking, and potential investigations. Because of the large volumes of information archived, an effective classification system that anticipates future uses is essential.

Destruction: Eventually the information will be destroyed because:

- The information is no longer deemed important, especially in comparison to the on-going storage costs. Although the cost of storage media continues to fall, the volumes of information being stored appears to be growing faster.
- Legislation, e.g. privacy laws, only allows the storage of information for a prescribed period.

Project reporting

One of the main duties of a project manager is to report on the status of the project; this is known as project reporting. In essence project reporting takes information about the project and presents it in an appropriate format to stakeholders and in line with the project communication plan. It is implied by the term 'reporting' that most reports are written (or in reality printed from computer software); however, reports can equally be verbal via progress meetings or conference calls.

Reporting tends to be a formal process with reports issued or presented either:

- in line with an agreed calendar, e.g. monthly
- at predetermined points in the life cycle, e.g. at the end of every phase
- after a significant activity has taken place.

The project manager will produce reports that cover topics such as progress against the schedule, expenditure against the budget and performance against the quality plan, the latest predicted end date and also against agreed key performance indicators (KPIs). There will also be reports produced as a result of audits, project reviews and risk assessments.

Reporting these things will give an indication of whether or not the project will deliver the required benefit, and if there is underperformance, remedial action can be taken before it is too late.

When reporting on projects it is often useful to consider a technique known as an **exception report**. This means that if everything is going to plan then almost nothing is said or written. Only when things are not going to plan, i.e. things are ahead or behind schedule, under spending or over spending, or quality is better or worse than planned, is a report made. Although reporting by exception is a means to reduce the burden of reporting, it requires a level of trust between the project manager and stakeholders that no news is good news and anything to the contrary will be reported and not ignored.

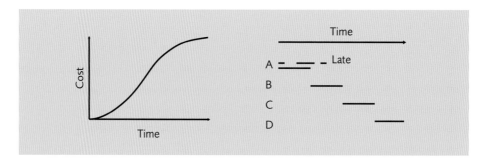

Figure 27.1 Reporting project status

Project Children's Hospice (PCH)

In the communication plan, you agreed with your boss (the sponsor) that you would meet on a formal one-to-one basis each week throughout the project. Your boss is aware of the principles of exception reporting and only wants you to update her on the things that are not going to plan at each weekly meeting.

You also have a weekly progress meeting with the project team. At this meeting you will present progress against the schedule and expenditure against the budget. In addition, you will also report how many hours have been booked against the project remembering you only have a budget of 1,000 hours to play with.

You will use the company's notice boards to report how much sponsor-ship money has been pledged to date. You intend to update this on a daily basis if the data can be made available.

Handover and closure (completion) phase

Introduction

In this section we look at the fourth and final phase on the project life cycle, the Handover and Closure phase. It is during this phase that the project is handed over to the customer or to 'business-as-usual' operations and brought to an administrative and physical close.

All completed projects should follow a procedural handover and closure in order to ensure that nothing has been missed and that all stakeholders are happy with the end results. Only when these activities are over can the project be deemed to be completed.

During project closure a post-project review should be carried out. One of the prime reasons for doing this is to ensure that appropriate lessons are learned and that the organisation's **knowledge management** requirements are properly met. This might not seem necessary for the project that has just been completed, but it is critical as an investment in the organisation's ability to improve the way projects are delivered to create future benefit.

Figure 28.1 Handover and Closure (completion) phase – overview

28

Handover and closure

Handover and Closure is the name given to the final phase in the project life cycle. During this phase the project outputs/deliverables are handed over to the sponsor and users, who are hopefully delighted with the results. Closure is the process of finishing the project and broadly covers two areas. First, administration, which could be seen as the boring part after all the excitement of the project, and second, learning for the future, which is hopefully seen as important and worthwhile.

Projects are used to deliver specific objectives for change. Just as projects need a controlled start and a controlled middle, they also need a controlled end.

At the completion of any project, the project manager must ensure that the deliverables or outputs are handed over to whoever is going to use them. In order to do this, it is beneficial for the project manager to follow an agreed handover and closure process.

Handover

Prior to **handover** the project manager must make sure that the project's deliverables meet the defined acceptance criteria. This may include formal testing or application of other quality controls. As a result of these tests or checks, the chance that the deliverables will be considered unacceptable by the end user will be minimised. Most project managers will require that the end user, either an external customer or the organisation's operational business, signs a certificate of acceptance to confirm that the deliverables have been handed over and meet requirements for use. This is important particularly to mark the official 'transfer of ownership' of deliverables, which can be critical for contractual purposes for some projects, or the passage of the asset on an organisation's balance sheet from an 'asset under construction' to an 'asset in use'.

Closure

During Closure the project manager must make sure that all project finance and general administration is completed. This will avoid the carry-over of work into operations and will formally signify the completion of the project. Administrative closure also requires settling any open claims on or from contractors. The project manager is also responsible for disbanding the project team and making sure that each team member, including contractors has finalised their work. The project manager must also conduct a post-project review, which is described as part of the next chapter.

In the event that a project is terminated early, it is also necessary to go through a formal closure process (handover is not necessary in this instance).

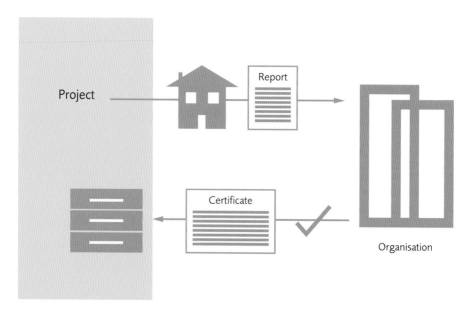

Figure 28.2 Project handover and closure

Project Children's Hospice (PCH)

Handover of the project will occur just prior to the presentation of the cheque to the fundraising manager of the Children's Hospice. When this point is reached it is important that the following checks have been made:

- All donations have been collected.
- There are no outstanding bills or invoices to be paid.
- All work is completed and no more company time will be used.

Handover will take place from the project manager to the sponsor. It will be the sponsor who makes the presentation to the charity.

29

Post-project reviews and knowledge management

All projects should undertake a post-project review (sometimes called a post-investment review or 'wash-up') to ensure that the experience of the project is recorded for the benefit of others, i.e. to learn lessons. This documented review of the project's performance is produced after the handover of deliverables is complete and during project closure but before the project is actually closed. It is another responsibility of the project manager.

Conducting a post-project review

In carrying out the review the project manager will seek to compare the final outcome of the project with the currently approved project success criteria that should be aligned in both the business case and PMP. If these criteria have all been met, the project should be considered a success. The project should not be closed until all project success criteria can be confirmed; however, this does not mean that all the benefits from the project will have been realised at closure. In such cases a benefits realisation review (see Chapter 26) should be planned at some later date, but this is the responsibility of the sponsor, not the project manager.

To complete the post-project review the project manager and other key members of the project team, such as the sponsor and members of the PMO, will need to look at other project documentation, such as:

- business case
- project management plan (PMP)
- risk log
- change log
- issue log
- project reports.

The importance of a post-project review

Post-project reviews allow the organisation to continuously improve by learning from experience. Some people would say that learning from experience prevents 'the same mistake being made twice' or 'reinventing the wheel at every opportunity'. Both of these statements imply that lessons to be learned from projects are always negative. This is clearly not the case. On most projects there are things that go right just as there are things that go wrong. It is important to understand both of these facets. It is even more important to understand what caused the things to go right and wrong, as the effect they had on the project will probably be quite obvious. Understanding the cause of something that went right will allow it to be done again; likewise, understanding the cause of something that went wrong will allow it to be avoided next time.

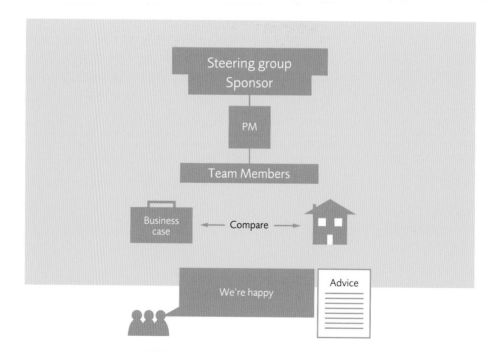

Figure 29.1 Post-project review

The following are examples of things that can be improved as a result of learning from experience:

- selection of suppliers
- identification of risks
- estimating accuracy for project and activity durations and costs
- resource deployment.

Some projects take a long time to complete. On such projects it is good practice to build a learning process into each project phase and not just wait until the end of the project when many people who have contributed may have moved on. The principles are the same – focus on the achievement of objectives and learn lessons for the future from what has gone well and where there is room for improvement. For many organisations this falls within the wider business principle and remit of continual improvement.

Project Children's Hospice (PCH)

As described in the chapter on project life cycle, the project will have gate reviews at the end of each phase. A short meeting was held with the sponsor once the event design and the PMP was complete and as a result of this some modifications were made to plans in order to meet the project success criteria for media coverage. It was useful to have this sanity check before pressing ahead with the communication phase of the project.

As project manager, it will be your responsibility to undertake a post-project review. In order for the review to be effective you should ensure that the following people attend:

- sponsor
- health and safety officer
- security adviser
- three games managers
- finance manager
- quality manager
- three 'representative event participants'.

As part of the review you will consider all the project documentation that has been prepared. One aim of the review will be for you to determine whether the project was a success or not by comparing the final outcome with the agreed project success criteria.

The other aim of the review will be for you to suggest how things could be improved if the company had a similar event in future.

A potential example of a lesson to be learned could be around the design of the sponsorship forms. You are considering delaying the start of this activity by one week. If you do this, it might mean that less money will be raised due to the shorter time between distributing the forms and the event. Should this risk occur, the underlying cause of the effect would have been that you wrongly re-prioritised this work rather than seeking assistance to make sure it happened as originally planned.

Knowledge management

When it comes to project management, post previews and knowledge management are closely related. The systematic management of information and learning is fundamental to any organisation that wants to continually improve the way it delivers its projects. Knowledge management turns personal information and experience gained during projects into collective knowledge that can be widely shared throughout an organisation and a profession. The lessons learned as part of a post-project review are fundamental to on-going knowledge management.

Extended and product life cycle phases

Introduction

As we explained in Chapter 4, a project life cycle must always include phases from the start of the work: Concept (initiation), through Definition (planning) and Development (execution or delivery), prior to Handover to the business or client and Closure of the project. Some organisations use an extended life cycle that takes in the organisational change-related work to put the project deliverables into operation and to realise and measure the benefits. Other organisations include this phase and also adopt a product-based life cycle through **Operations** to eventual termination and disposal of the asset.

In this section we briefly consider some of the key points associated with benefit realisation and measurement (the extended life cycle) and operations and termination (the **product life cycle**).

30

Extended and product life cycle phases

Benefit realisation and measurement

Benefits are the measurable outcomes of projects that are of value to stakeholders. It is quite possible that a project, either intentionally or unintentionally, delivers outcomes that are not of value to stakeholders. These are typically called dis-benefits. An example might be that during a project to increase the efficiency of operations the good-will that had previously been built up between operators and management in a manufacturing plan is damaged. The project delivered its financial business case (cost savings) but there was a reduction in staff satisfaction when this was measured through the annual employee engagement process. During project delivery, the risk of delivering dis-benefits needs to be closely monitored.

Organisational change management

Delivering desired benefits almost always necessitates delivering changed ways of working for the people in the business (the users). When we were discussing benefits in an early chapter we said that, increasingly, organisational change-related scope is included in the project scope, so the project not only delivers technical outputs but also the changed outcomes for the business. When we wrote the first edition of this book more than 10 years ago, this was rarely the case. Projects were seen as vehicles to deliver technical outputs and wider business change, and benefits realisation was delivered by programme manage-ment. Programmes still deliver benefits, but the boundaries between projects and programmes have become blurred in this respect. So without getting into a debate about whether projects or programmes deliver business transformation and benefits, it is best to just be aware that some projects do. Where it is the case that projects include an element of business transformation, it is important to:

Starting Out in Project Management

- closely involve representatives of the business in the project, not just providing them with information, but including them in decision making
- consider how people deal with the change and the reasons why some people might seem to be resisting change
- provide multiple and different ways for the recipients of change to understand what is going on and to get involved, through information sharing, pilots and early adoption of parts of the scope (if this is possible).

In some sectors, projects continue to be mainly technical endeavours – to build roads, railways, buildings, plant and equipment or for product development purposes. In most organisations, however, project-based working is used for all sorts of other changes – from information systems development to wider organisation design and development. In all cases, but especially when the project outputs and outcomes are less physical and where project success is more subjective, it is important that project scope includes work to get the business ready to accept, use and realise benefit from the change.

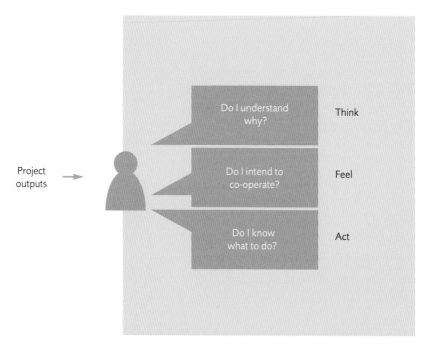

Figure 30.1 Organisational change management

Benefits tracking

Benefits are the measurable outcomes of projects. The type and scale of benefits desired is a key part of the business case – used to justify the investment in the project. You may hear stories that in reality the benefits are only needed to get the business case approved and that no one will attempt to measure benefits once the project is completed. This used to be the case, but increasingly organisations are demanding more and expect to be able to justify the return on investment from change.

To track benefits over time, it is clearly necessary to have a good understanding of the measurement baseline, the 'current state' of the measure that you are looking to improve. This may be the operational cost base, the revenue from a particular line of business, the customer satisfaction survey or the safety performance of the business. The person responsible for tracking benefits must agree the baseline with senior stakeholders and, as part of this, make it clear what variables, other than project delivery, might affect the benefit measures. Clear attribution of the project outputs to benefits is vital.

Once measurement baselines and methods of tracking are defined, the project manager can then report each month. It is usually useful to start tracking the benefits during development of the project to see how the parameters fluctuate without the implementation of change.

Benefits realisation reviews

In the Handover and Closure phase of the project life cycle, it is good practice to complete a post-project review to learn lessons from the project. Where an organisation has an extended life cycle to include the tracking of benefit realisation post handover, it is normal for a benefit realisation review to be the formal input to the project closure gate.

Operations

It would be trivial to say that in the Operations phase of the project whatever has been created will be operated, but that is the case. For example, the new IT system will be used, the motorway will have cars and lorries driven on it or the new procedure will be enacted. It should be obvious that in many instances the Operations phase will be far longer than the phases that make up the 'creation' of the asset. This is certainly the case when it comes to motorways and other large capital assets. It is during the Operations phase that the asset will also need to be maintained, sometimes triggering a new project to carry out non-routine maintenance that may be necessary from time to time.

Termination

In many environments the need to terminate and dispose of assets is now becoming a reality, e.g. North Sea oil platforms and nuclear power stations. The costs of terminating and disposing of these assets were always considered, but the eventual magnitude of the outgoing was never really appreciated. Of course, in many business sectors the cost of termination and disposal is largely irrelevant and is often borne by others, e.g. the termination and disposal of a high-rise building or office block.

Total cost of ownership

The reason why operations and termination is considered important is to establish the total cost of ownership of an asset. This is often called 'whole life costing' or 'through life costing'. The total cost of ownership includes the capital expended on creating the asset, the cost of operations and maintenance and the cost of termination and disposal. Of course, the revenue or income generated by the asset also needs to be taken into account in order to offset the outgoings. In many examples of projects to change organisations, e.g. to make the organisation more efficient, rather than to build a revenue earning assets, the 'income' will be in the form of cost avoidance.

Looking at the complete life cycle of the project will sometimes impact the solution that is chosen. The decision to choose a solution that is cheap to create but expensive to operate versus a solution that is expensive to create and cheap to operate is often a difficult choice and will depend on many factors. This should be considered as early as possible in the life cycle, and definitely before the design is finalised and the final investment decision is made for the project.

Glossary

Acceptance criteria   The requirements and essential conditions that have to be achieved before project deliverables are accepted.

Activity
1: a task, job, operation or process consuming time and possibly other resources.
2: the smallest self-contained unit of work used to define the logic of the project.

Actual cost (AC)   The total costs actually incurred (paid or accrued) and recorded in accomplishing work performed during a given time period. Also known as Actual Cost of Work Performed (ACWP).

Agile   A family of development methodologies where requirements and solutions are developed iteratively and incrementally throughout the project life cycle.

Assumptions   Statements that will be taken for granted as fact and upon which the project business case will be justified.

Baseline   The reference levels against which a project is monitored and controlled – can apply to schedules, budget and requirements.

Benefit   The quantifiable and measurable improvement resulting from completion of deliverables that is perceived as positive by a stakeholder. It will normally have a tangible value, expressed in monetary terms that will justify the investment.

Benefits realisation   The practice of ensuring that benefits are derived from the outputs and outcomes of the project. Also, the life cycle phase during which benefits are realised.

Bottom-up estimating   An estimating technique that uses detailed specification to estimate time and cost for each product or activity. Sometimes called analytical estimating.

Budget   The agreed cost of the project or a quantification of resources needed to achieve an activity by a set time. It is agreed at the end of the initial estimating process.

Glossary

Business case   Provides justification for undertaking a project or programme. It evaluates the benefit, cost and risk of alternative options and provides a rationale for the preferred solution. It is owned by the sponsor and is often created by the project or programme manager.

Business-as-usual   An organisation's normal day-to-day operations.

Change control (process)   A process that ensures that all requests to change the baseline scope of a project, programme or portfolio are captured, evaluated and then approved, rejected or deferred, and implemented if approved.

Change freeze   A point after which no further changes to scope will be considered.

Change log (register)   A record of proposed, evaluated and implemented changes to the scope.

Change request   A request to obtain formal approval for project changes to the scope of the work.

Commitment   The placement of an order for work to be done and the amount of money ring-fenced or removed from the budget represented by this order.

Communication   The means by which information or instructions are exchanged. It is successful when the received meaning is the same as the transmitted meaning.

Communication plan   A document that identifies what information is to be transmitted to whom, why, when, where, how, through which medium and the desired impact.

Comparative estimating   An estimating technique based on the comparison with, and factoring from, the cost of a previous work. Sometimes called analogous estimating.

Concept   The first phase of the project or programme life cycle. During this phase the need, opportunity or problem is confirmed, the overall feasibility of the project is considered and a preferred solution identified.

Configuration   The set of functional and physical characteristics of a final deliverable defined in specification and achieved in the execution of plans.

Configuration management   The administrative activities concerned with the creation, maintenance, controlled change and quality control of the scope of work.

Conflict management   The process of identifying and addressing differences that, if left unresolved, could affect objectives, by allowing natural differences to become destructive. Different positions/styles can be adopted depending on the circumstances.

Conflict-Mode Instrument (Thomas and Kilman)   Competing, accommodating, collaborating, avoiding and compromising. Conflict handling modes can also be considered as conflict management styles.

Constraints   Things that should be considered as fixed or that must happen. Restrictions that will affect the project.

Consumable (resource)   A type or resource that only remains available until consumed (e.g. a material).

Context   A collective term for the governance and setting of a project, programme or portfolio.

Contingency   Resource set aside for responding to identified risk. Planned allocation of time, cost or other resources held in case they are needed to manage unforeseen or accepted risks, both opportunities and threats.

Continual improvement   A business philosophy (known in Japan as Kaizen) used to systematically improve an aspect of business by focusing on goals and priorities.

Contract   An agreement made between two or more parties that creates legally binding obligations between them. It sets out those obligations and the actions that can be taken if they are not met.

Cost breakdown structure (CBS)   A hierarchical way to define cost elements for the project.

Critical chain   An alternative method of scheduling projects – alternatively called resource critical path – that reduces multi-tasking and builds buffers into a schedule to protect progress.

Critical path   A sequence of activities through a network diagram from start to finish, the sum of whose durations determines the overall duration. There may be more than one such path.

Critical path analysis   The procedure for calculating the critical path and floats in a network diagram.

Glossary

Critical success factors (CSF)   Success factors that, if absent, would cause the project, programme or portfolio to fail.

Definition   The second phase of a project or programme life cycle where requirements are refined, the preferred solution is identified, and ways of achieving it are identified.

Deliverable   A product, set of products or a package that will be delivered to, and formally accepted by a stakeholder. In this sense, a stakeholder can be anyone involved in the project. Note that in project management deliverable and product are synonyms and therefore are used interchangeably.

Development   The third phase of the project life cycle, where the project management plan is executed, monitored and controlled. It may be broken down into further stages to assist management.

Earned value (EV)   The value of completed work expressed in terms of budget assigned to that work. A measure of progress that may be expressed in cost or labour terms. Also known as Budgeted Cost of Work Performed (BCWP).

Earned value management (EVM)   A project control process, based on a structured approach to planning, cost collection and performance measurement. It facilitates the integration of project scope, time and cost, risk and recourse objectives and the establishment of a baseline plan of performance measurement.

Environment   The circumstances and conditions within which the project, programme or portfolio must operate. In this instance, the term environment does not relate to the world in which we live.

Escalation   The process by which issues are drawn to the attention of a higher level of management. This enables decisions to be taken at the appropriate level such that the issue can be managed.

Estimate   An approximation of time and cost targets, refined throughout the life cycle. Can also apply to resources and benefits.

Estimate at completion (EAC)   The forecasted total cost of the project using cost efficiency to date.

Estimating funnel   A representation of the increasing levels of estimating accuracy that can be achieved through the phases of the life cycle by understanding and managing risk.

Exception report   A focused report drawing attention to instances where actual results are expected to be, or are already, outside the agreed tolerance.

Extended life cycle   A life cycle model that includes the operation of outputs and the realisation of benefits.

Fixed price (contract)   A term of payment where the amount of money to be paid for a fixed scope is agreed in advance. Rigorous scope definition and change control is required if this type of contract payment is used.

Float   A term used to describe the flexibility with which an activity may be rescheduled. There are various types of float, such as total float and free float.

Free float   The time by which an activity may be delayed or extended without affecting the start of any succeeding activity.

Functional organisation (structure)   Where specific functions of a business e.g. finance or HR are grouped together to provide a dedicated service to the whole. In such a situation, a project manager has little authority over project staff, who report into the functional manager.

Funding   This is the means by which the capital required to undertake a project, programme or portfolio, is secured and then made available as required.

Gantt (bar) chart   A graphical representation of activity against time. Variations may include information such as 'actual vs. planned', resource usage and dependencies.

Gate review   A formal point in a project where the expected worth, progress, cost and execution plans are reviewed and a decision is made whether to continue (go or no-go) with the next phase of the project.

Gate   The point between phases, gates and/or tranches where go/no go decision can be made about the remainder of the work.

Governance   The set of policies, regulations, functions, processes, procedures and responsibilities that define the establishment, management and control of projects, programmes or portfolios.

Handover and Closure   This is the fourth and final phase of the project life cycle. The final deliverables are transferred to the sponsor and the end users. This is followed by the formal end point of a project, either because it has been completed or because it has been terminated early. It is where all project matters, carrying out final project reviews, archiving information and redeploying the remaining project team takes place.

Health and safety management The process of identifying and minimising threats to workers and those affected by the work throughout the project, programme or portfolio life cycle. Note this also includes both security and environmental aspects.

Information management The collection, storage, dissemination, archiving and appropriate destruction of project information. It enables teams and stakeholders to use their time, resources and expertise effectively to make decisions and to fulfil their roles.

Internal rate of return (IRR) The discount rate at which the net present value of an investment would be zero. Enables decisions to be taken about whether the investment is worth it or not by comparing the IRR to the rate the cash could earn elsewhere. Makes it possible to make allowances for how the value of money changes over time. Money today is of more value than money in the future; you can today's money to make more money, or at the very least invest the money to get the interest.

Issue This occurs when the tolerances for delegated work are exceeded. This triggers the escalation of the matter from one level of management to the next in order to seek a solution.

Issue log (register) A formal record of all issues and their status.

Issue management The process by which issues that are impacting the project objectives, and cannot be resolved by the project manager alone, are identified. Issues are escalated to allow them to be addressed by the next level of management.

Key performance indicators (KPI) Measures of success that can be used throughout the project, programme or portfolio to ensure that it is progressing towards a successful conclusion.

Knowledge management The systematic management of information and learning. It turns personal information and experience into collective knowledge that can be widely shared throughout an organisation and a profession.

Leadership The ability to establish vision and direction, to influence and align others towards a common purpose, and to empower and inspire people to achieve success.

Lessons learned   Documented experiences that can be used to improve the future management of projects, programmes and portfolios.

Life cycle   The inter-related phases of a project, programme or portfolio and provides a structure for governing the progression of work.

Life cycle cost   The total cost of a project over its whole extended/product life cycle. Used to look at costs of commissioning, operation and disposal, not just development. Often called whole-life cost.

Make or buy (decision)   This is the act of choosing between manufacturing a product in-house or purchasing it from an external supplier. The two most important factors are cost and availability of production capacity.

Management reserve   A sum of money held as an overall contingency to cover the cost impact of some unexpected event. Held by the board of a company to cover the cost impact of risk at a realistic level for all project, programmes or portfolios undertaken by the company.

Matrix organisation structure   Where the project manager and functional managers share responsibility for assigning priorities and for directing work.

Method   Embodies best practice and provides consistent guidelines for people involved in projects, programmes and portfolios. Some organisations use their own bespoke approach, while others use approaches that are publically available, such as PRINCE2®, MSP® and MoP®.

Milestone   A key event selected for its importance in the project.

Negotiation   A discussion between two or more parties aimed at reaching agreement, through seeking acceptance, consensus and/or the alignment of views. Negotiation happens on an informal basis throughout the project life cycle and on a formal basis such as during procurement.

Negotiation process   Planning, discussing, proposing, bargaining and agreement (and review).

Net present value (NPV)   The sum of future net cashflows discounted back to a common base date. The sum of discounted cashflows for each period being considered by the investment.

Objectives   Predetermined results towards which effort is directed. Objectives may be defined in terms of outputs, outcomes and/or benefits.

Glossary

Operations The life cycle phase during which changes to the way people work with the new product, service or procedure is managed. The results are monitored and reported to ensure the financial or other benefits are achieved in line with the original business case.

Organisational breakdown structure (OBS) A hierarchical way in which the project organisation may be divided into management levels and groups, for planning and control purposes.

Outcomes The changed circumstances or behaviour that results from the use of an output.

Outputs The tangible or intangible products typically delivered by a project.

Parametric estimating An estimating technique that uses a statistical relationship between historic data and other variables to calculate an estimate.

Partnering (and alliancing) A type of contractual arrangement where the parties agree to share ideas and information to improve the performance and results for everyone using a win–win approach.

Payback The period of time it is predicted that a project or programme will take to return the original investment. Can be done on a straight cash in/cash out basis, or using discounted cashflows.

Peer review This is an internal assessment, conducted by a member of your organisation with a similar background and experience of this project topic, similar to yours. May be requested by a senior manager/sponsor.

PESTLE A technique for analysing project context by considering political, economic, sociological, technical, legal and environmental factors.

Phase The major subdivision of a life cycle.

Planned cost (PC) The authorised budget assigned to the scheduled work to be completed. The total planned cost is also known as budget at completion (BAC) or Budgeted Cost of Work Scheduled (BCWS).

Portfolio A grouping of an organisation's projects and programmes that can be managed at an organisational or functional level.

Portfolio management The selection, prioritisation and control of an organisation's projects and programmes in line with its strategic objectives and capacity to deliver.

Post-project review   Undertaken after the project deliverables have been handed over and before final closeout, this review is intended to produce lessons learned that will enable continuous improvement.

Procedure   Sets out the generally sequential steps to follow in order to perform (project) management processes. It describes how to document each step of the process, what parameters should be associated with it and how much detailing is required.

Process   Defines the overall end-to-end steps involved in the execution of a project policy and the main steps required. It describes the tools to be used, people to contact and all the other relevant information.

Procurement   The process by which products and services are acquired from an external provider for incorporation into the project, programme or portfolio.

Procurement strategy   A strategy that sets out how to acquire and manage resources (goods and services) required by a project, programme or portfolio. It will also include aspects such as selection strategy, types of contract and reimbursement methods.

Product breakdown structure (PBS)   A hierarchy of deliverables (products) that are required to be produced on the project.

Product life cycle   A life cycle that begins at the start of the Concept phase, and continues until the final act of decommissioning/disposal of a product or service at the end of the Termination phase.

Program evaluation and review technique (PERT)   A network analysis technique that calculates standard deviation for the schedule based on three point estimates of activity duration. A formula that calculates the weighted average time and/or cost outcomes of an activity by taking into consideration a three-point estimate (Best Case + 4 times Most Likely + Worst Case – all divided by 6).

Programme   A group of related projects and change management activities that together achieve a beneficial change of a strategic nature for an organisation.

Programme management   The coordinated management of projects and change management activities to achieve beneficial change.

Project   A unique, transient endeavour undertaken to achieve a desired outcome.

Glossary

Project change   A modification to the project's baseline scope and/or cost, time or quality objectives.

Project evaluation review   A document review of the project performance produced at predefined points in each phase of the project life cycle. Directed, scheduled and chaired by the project manager.

Project life cycle   Four phases – concept, definition, development and handover and closure.

Project management   The application of processes, methods, knowledge, skills and experience to achieve the project objectives.

Project management plan (PMP)   The output of the definition phase of a project. The document that brings together all the plans for the project. It becomes the reference document for managing the project. It is owned by the project manager and is created by the project manager, team members and subject-matter experts.

Project management process   The generic set of processes that need to apply to each phase of the project life cycle.

Project manager   The individual responsible for the successful delivery of the project.

Project office   A group of people who work in a function designed to support project management by providing information and specialist advice to managers. Also referred to as the information hub for the project. Often the custodian of project management methods and procedures. Sometimes called a project support office (PSO) or project management office (PMO). A programme office does the same thing for a programme.

Project organisation structure   When functions, e.g. finance or HR are integrated within projects to provide the maximum authority to the project manager.

Project risk (overall project risk)   The collective effect of estimating uncertainty and risk events on project objectives.

Project team   A set of individuals, groups and/or organisations responsible to the project manager for working towards a common purpose.

Quality   The fitness for purpose or the degree of conformance of the outputs of the process or the process itself.

Quality assurance   The process of evaluating overall project performance on a regular basis to provide confidence that the project will satisfy the relevant quality standards.

Quality control   The process of monitoring specific work results to determine if they comply with relevant quality standards and specifications, and to identify ways in which to eliminate causes of unsatisfactory performance.

Quality management   A discipline for ensuring the outputs, benefits and the processes by which they are delivered, meet stakeholder requirements and are fit for purpose.

Quality planning   The process of determining which quality standards are necessary and how to apply them.

Re-usable (resource)   A resource that when no longer needed becomes available for other uses. Accommodation, machines, test equipment and people are re-usable.

Reporting   Taking information and presenting it in an appropriate format, which includes the formal communication of project information to stakeholders.

Requirements   The clear and agreed expression of stakeholder and user wants and needs with a focus on what is necessary not how it will be achieved. They should be comprehensive, clear, well structured, traceable and testable.

Requirements management   The process of capturing, assessing and justifying stakeholders' wants and needs. Once agreed, requirements should be baselined.

Resource histogram   A view of project data in which resource requirements, usage and availability are shown using vertical bars against a horizontal timescale.

Resource levelling   A scheduling calculation that delays activities such that resource usage is kept below specified limits. It is also known as resource limited scheduling.

Resource management   The acquisition and deployment of the internal and external resources required to deliver the project, programme or portfolio.

Resource smoothing   A scheduling calculation that involves utilising float or increasing or decreasing the resources required for specific activities, such that any peaks and troughs of resource usage are smoothed out. This does not affect the overall duration. It is also known as time-limited resource scheduling.

Glossary

Resources   All those items required to undertake work including people, finance and materials.

Responsibility assignment matrix (RAM)   A diagram or chart showing assigned responsibilities for elements of work. It is created by combining the work breakdown structure (WBS), with the organisational breakdown structure (OBS).

Risk (event)   An uncertain event or set of circumstances that would, if it occurred, have an effect on the achievement of one or more of the project objectives.

Risk log (register)   A document listing identified risk events and their corresponding planned responses.

Risk management   A process that allows individual risk events and overall risk to be understood and managed proactively, optimising success by minimising threats and maximising opportunities.

Risk management process   Initiate, identify, assess, plan a response and implement it. This is a five-step process, which allows all aspects of risk to be addressed, at an appropriate level, if the organisation requires it.

Risk owner   The person best placed to monitor and respond to an identified risk.

Risk response   An action or set of actions to reduce the probability or the impact of a threat, or to increase the probability or impact of an opportunity.

'S' curve   A graphical display of cumulative costs, labour hours or other quantities, plotted against time. The profile of expenditure on a project tends to be slower at the beginning and end and faster in the middle. It is the graphical view of planned expenditure or planned cost.

Schedule   A timetable showing the forecast start and finish dates for activities or events within a project, programme or portfolio.

Scope   The totality of the outputs, outcomes and benefits and the work required to produce them.

Scope creep   The effect of allowing on-going changes to project scope and/or requirements without effective change control. The impact is that more scope is expected without the necessary increase in time and budget to accommodate it.

Scope management   The process whereby outputs, outcomes and benefits are identified, defined and controlled.

Situational leadership   The term used to convey that an effective leader would be expected to be able to use a range of styles to motivate others towards goal achievement.

Sponsor   The individual for whom the project or programme is undertaken and who is the primary risk taker. They also ensure that the project or programme remains a viable proposition and that benefits are realised.

Sponsorship   An important, active senior management role. It ensures that the work is governed effectively and delivers the objectives that meet identified needs.

Stakeholder   The organisations or people who have an interest or role in the project, programme or portfolio, or are impacted by it.

Stakeholder analysis   The identification of stakeholders and stakeholder groups, their interests, attitude and ability to influence the project, programme or portfolio. It will also consider the manner in which stakeholders are impacted.

Stakeholder engagement   The systematic identification, analysis, planning and implementation of actions designed to engage with stakeholders.

Steering group/committee   A group, usually comprising the sponsor, senior managers and sometimes key stakeholders, whose remit is to set the strategic direction of a project (sometimes called project board).

Sub-contract   A type of contract where the supplier is responsible for a specific part of the project scope and where a number of different sub-contractors are likely to be used in parallel.

Success criteria   The qualitative or quantitative measures by which the success of project, programme and portfolio management is judged.

Success factors   Management practices that, when implemented, will increase the likelihood of success of a project, programme or portfolio. The degree to which these practices are established and embedded within an organisation indicates its level of maturity.

Glossary

Supplier   A contractor, consultant or any organisation which provides resources to the project (sometimes called a provider).

Sustainability   An environmental, social and economically integrated approach to development that meets present needs without compromising the environment for future generations.

Team development   The process of developing knowledge and skills, as a group and individually, that enhance performance.

Team member   A person who is accountable to and has work assigned to them by the project manager to be performed either by them or by others in a working group.

Teamwork   The action of a group of people working in collaboration or by cooperation towards a common goal.

Termination   The decommissioning and disposal of a deliverable at the end of its useful life.

Thomas-Kilmann Conflict Mode Instrument   This instrument describes five conflict handing modes – competing, accommodating, collaborating, avoiding and compromising. Conflict handling modes can also be considered as conflict management styles.

Three-point estimate   An estimate in which optimistic, most likely and pessimistic values are given. This reflects the risks associated with the work by estimating the best case, worst case and most likely time and/or cost outcomes, rather than just a single point.

Tolerance   A permissible variation in performance parameters.

Total float   Time by which an activity may be delayed or extended without affecting the overall duration or violating a target finish date.

Tranche   A sub-division of the project delivery phase of a programme created to facilitate approval gates at suitable points in the programme life cycle.

Tuckman team-development model   Originated by Bruce Tuckman using the concepts of forming, storming, norming, performing and adjourning.

Users   The group of people who are intended to receive the benefits or operate outputs – sometimes called end users.

Waterfall   A type of life cycle where the phases are sequential. Sometimes called a linear life cycle.

Work breakdown structure (WBS)   A hierarchy of work that is required to be done to achieve the project objectives.

Work package   A group of related activities that are defined at the same level within a work breakdown structure (WBS).

Index

Index